WORLD BOOK'S
YOUNG SCIENTIST

WORLD BOOK'S

YOUNG SCIENTIST

Volume 7

World Book, Inc.
a Scott Fetzer company
Chicago   London   Sydney   Toronto

Activities that have this warning symbol require some adult supervision!

The quest to explore the known world and to describe its creation and subsequent development is nearly as old as mankind. In the Western world, the best-known creation story comes from the book of Genesis. It tells how God created the earth and all living things. Modern religious thinkers interpret the Biblical story of creation in various ways. Some believe that creation occurred exactly as Genesis describes it. Others think that God's method of creation is revealed through scientific investigation. *Young Scientist* presents an exciting picture of what scientists have learned about life and the universe.

1993 Revised Printing

© 1991, 1990 World Book, Inc. All rights reserved. This volume may not be reproduced in whole or in part in any form without prior written permission from the publisher.

World Book, Inc.
525 W. Monroe
Chicago, IL 60661

ISBN: 0-7166-2794-9
Library of Congress Catalog Card No. 93-60294

Printed in the United States of America

G/IC

Contents

HUMAN BODY

Your living body

People are of different shapes and sizes — and different colors, too. Some are tall, some are short, and others are somewhere in between. Some have curly hair, some straight hair. Skin can be dark or light brown, yellowish or pinkish-white. Eyes can be brown, blue, green, or gray.

Sometimes people look like each other, especially if they are from the same family. They are even more alike if they are identical twins. But no two people are exactly the same. Everyone has his or her own special shape and unique fingerprints, footprints, and voice.

Inside your body

In many ways, your body is like a wonderful machine. Each of the many different parts of your body has a special job to do. Your bones and muscles work together to make you move. Your heart pumps blood around your body. Your lungs take in a gas called oxygen from the air. The most complicated part of your body is your brain, which controls all the other parts. Along with your nervous system, your brain keeps your body working.

Machines need fuel to make them work. For example, cars need gasoline. The fuel for the human machine is food. You need a regular supply of food to keep your body working properly.

Of course, you're not really a machine because you're alive. You have a living body. You grow like other living things do. But no other kind of animal can think, feel, and talk like you can. You are a unique living thing.

Scientists have made a robot that plays a keyboard. But they cannot make a machine that is able to do all the things that a human being can do.

Find out more by looking at
pages **20–21**
40–41

This photograph shows three nerve cells in a human brain. The branches coming out from the cells carry messages to other parts of the body.

What's your body made of?

Like all other living things, your body is made of tiny parts called **cells.** Most cells are so small that you can see them only with the help of a microscope. There are many trillions of cells in your body. Your skin, blood, muscles, and most other parts of you are made of cells.

Cells are made of a jellylike substance called **cytoplasm** and a nucleus. Cells are alive. They make new cells by dividing in two. Every day, your body makes about two billion new cells, but at the same time about two billion old cells die. This helps your body to keep itself in good working order.

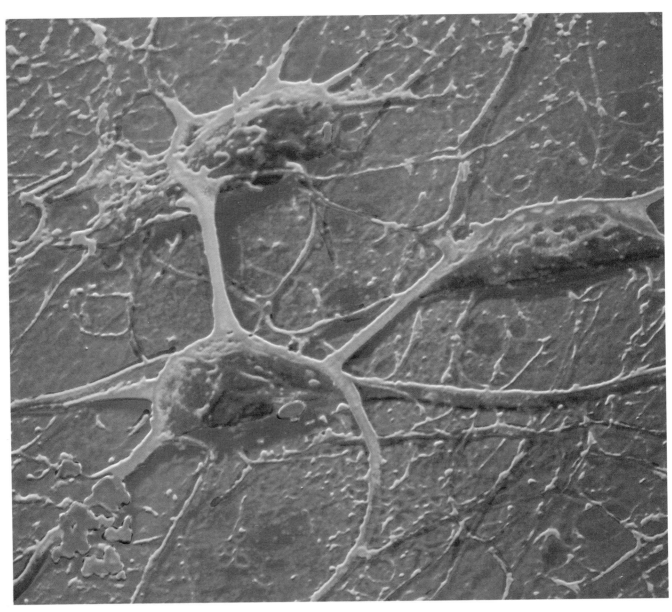

Different cells have different jobs

Cells have different shapes and sizes because they do different jobs. The cells in your muscles are long and stretchy. Many blood cells are round. Nerve cells are long and thin, with lots of branches like a tree. Nerve cells carry messages to and from your brain.

Cells of the same kind and function join together to make a material called **tissue.** Different kinds of tissue join together to make parts of your body called **organs.** You have many different organs, such as your eyes, your heart, and your brain.

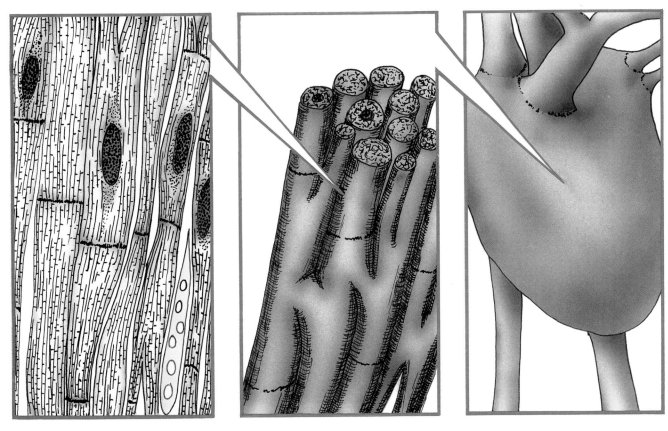

1. Long, stretchy muscle cells are grouped together.

2. Muscle cells join together to form muscle tissue. This consists of bunches of threadlike fibers.

3. Muscle tissues like this make up the walls of the heart. This organ pumps blood all around your body.

How much of your body is water?

About two-thirds of your body is made up of water. This lies in and around your tissues and organs.

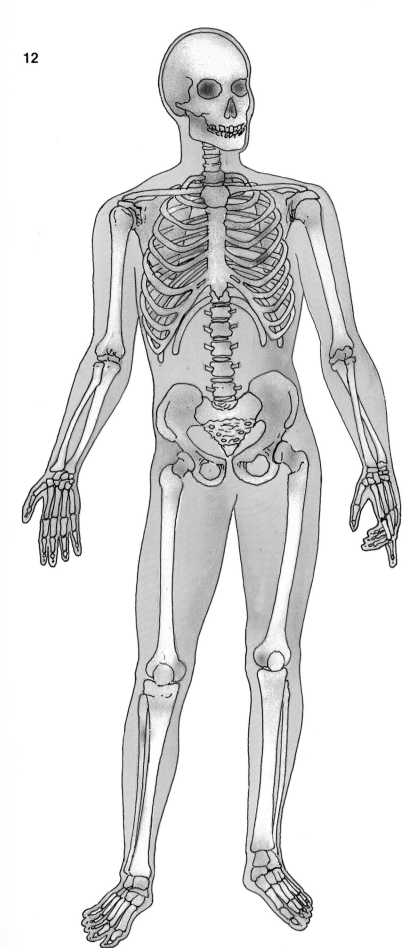

12

Your body's framework

You have about 200 bones in your body. They are joined together to make up the **skeleton.** Your skeleton helps give your body its shape. The bones of your skull determine the shape of your head. Long bones hold muscles that shape your arms and legs. Rib bones curve to make the sides of your chest. Your skeleton is the framework of your body. It holds you up and also helps you to move around.

Some bones protect your main inner organs. For example, your skull protects your brain. And your ribs make a rib cage around your heart and lungs.

What are bones made of?

Bones are hard tissues that are living parts of your body, just as your brain and heart are living parts. Bones contain cells that divide and multiply, causing you to grow. These cells are also always rebuilding the bony tissue to keep it strong. Rebuilding happens less as people grow older. So a broken bone will often heal much more quickly in a child than in an adult.

Bones store substances called **minerals,** which your body uses. Calcium is a mineral. It helps to make the bones hard.

Bones have a strong covering, called **periosteum.** Inside, there is a hard layer of **compact bone.** A long bone, such as the thigh bone, has spongy tissue at its ends, called **cancellous bone,** and soft **marrow** in its hollow center.

Some parts of your skeleton, such as your arms and legs, have only a few long bones. Other parts, such as your hands and feet, have many small bones.

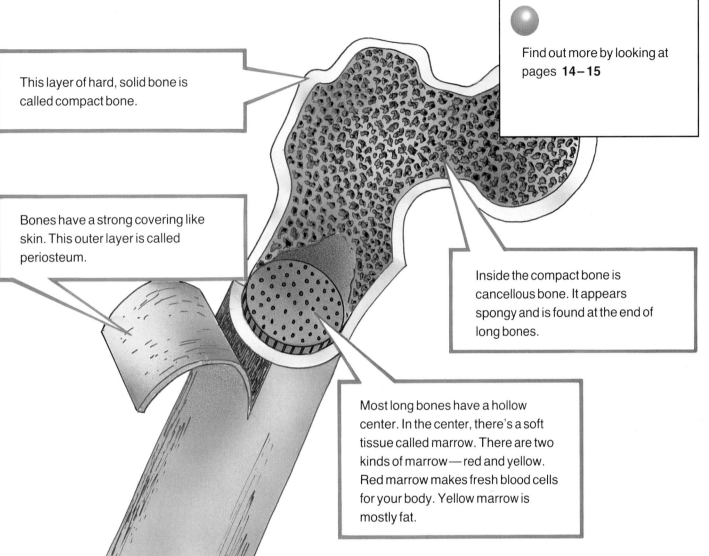

This layer of hard, solid bone is called compact bone.

Find out more by looking at pages **14–15**

Bones have a strong covering like skin. This outer layer is called periosteum.

Inside the compact bone is cancellous bone. It appears spongy and is found at the end of long bones.

Most long bones have a hollow center. In the center, there's a soft tissue called marrow. There are two kinds of marrow—red and yellow. Red marrow makes fresh blood cells for your body. Yellow marrow is mostly fat.

How are bones held together?

Your bones are held together by strong, flexible straps called **ligaments.** The ends of the bones are covered with a smooth, rubbery substance called **cartilage.** This is the same kind of substance that forms the tip of your nose. Cartilage works like a cushion so that the bones don't grind against each other. Cartilage is covered in a liquid called **synovial fluid.** This keeps the bones moving smoothly, like oil in the parts of a machine.

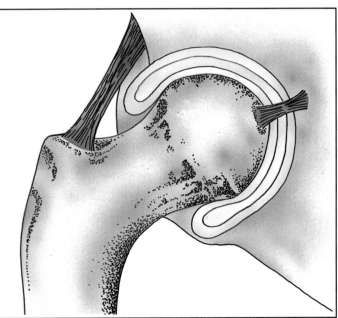

Find out more by looking at
pages **10–11**
   20–21
   22–23

14

On the move

Your body moves in many different ways. You can bend, stretch, turn, and twist. You can move because your bones move at your **joints,** places where your bones meet. But your bones can't move by themselves — they need something to pull at them. This job is done by your muscles, which are joined to your bones in order to move them.

Joints

There are many joints that help your body move. When you turn your head, bend your knees, or twist your wrists, your joints are in action. Some joints, such as those in your skull, do not move. These are called **fixed joints.** Each of the other kinds of joints does a specific type of movement.

Different kinds of joints

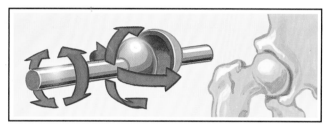

Ball and socket joints give you the most movement. The round end of one bone fits into a hollow part of another bone. Examples are your hip joints and shoulder joints.

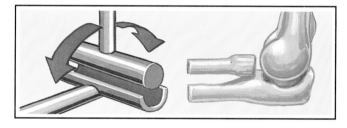

Hinge joints work like a door on a hinge. Movement in hinge joints is only in two directions. Your knees and elbows have hinge joints.

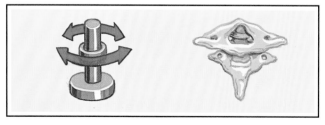

Pivot joints allow parts of your body to twist. Your head moves from side to side because it rests on a pivot joint at the top of your spine. In the same way, you can turn your hands over by flipping your wrists.

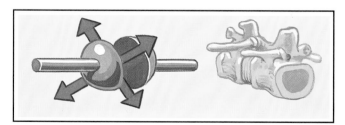

Gliding joints are one of the simplest kinds of joints. They allow a sliding movement when two pieces of bone come together. There are gliding joints on your backbone where the ribs meet the vertebrae.

Different kinds of muscle

There are more than 600 major muscles in your body. Not all are joined to your bones. For example, muscles line your blood vessels to keep blood flowing. Your lungs work because of regular muscle movement.

Some muscles move only when you decide to stand up, sit down, or move in other ways. These are the **voluntary muscles** that are joined to your bones. There are other muscles that work without your thinking about them. These **involuntary muscles** are made of smooth muscle fibers. They mash the food material in your stomach and then act to move it along through your intestines. Your heart is made of another special kind of muscle called **cardiac muscle.** It moves in a regular rhythm as it pumps blood to all parts of your body.

How do muscles work?

Muscles are made of tough, elastic tissue. They are built so that they can **contract,** which means that they become shorter. When the muscles whose ends are joined to bones contract, they pull at the bones and make them move.

Muscles are made up of long, thin cells that join together to make muscle fibers. When the muscle becomes shorter, all the fibers move closer together, making the muscle bulge. You can see your muscles bulging and relaxing when you move your arms and legs. If you bend your elbow and clench your fist, the muscles called **biceps** in your upper arm will bulge.

Muscles can only pull — they can't push. Muscles whose ends are joined to bones work in pairs. One muscle contracts and pulls the bone one way, and the other contracts to pull the bone back again.

When you tighten your biceps muscle, you bend your arm. When the other big muscle in your arm, the triceps, tightens, your arm straightens out again.

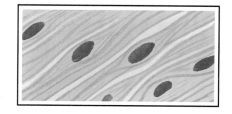

Smooth muscle is found in the stomach, in the intestines, and in the walls of blood vessels.

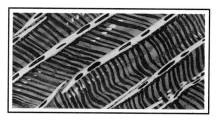

Striped muscles are the muscles that make your body move. They are attached to the bones.

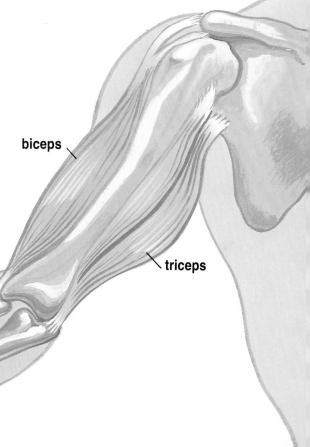

biceps

triceps

Find out more by looking at pages **18–19**

In and out

As you breathe, your chest moves in and out, and up and down. Inside your chest, there are two flexible, spongelike organs on either side of your heart. These are your **lungs.** When we **inhale** (take in air), we breathe in **oxygen,** a gas which helps to give us energy. When we **exhale** (expel air), we breathe out **carbon dioxide,** a harmful waste gas.

When you breathe in, your lungs fill with air and become larger. When you breathe out, your lungs become smaller as gas is squeezed out of them.

You breathe air in through your mouth and nose so that you can take in the oxygen your body needs.

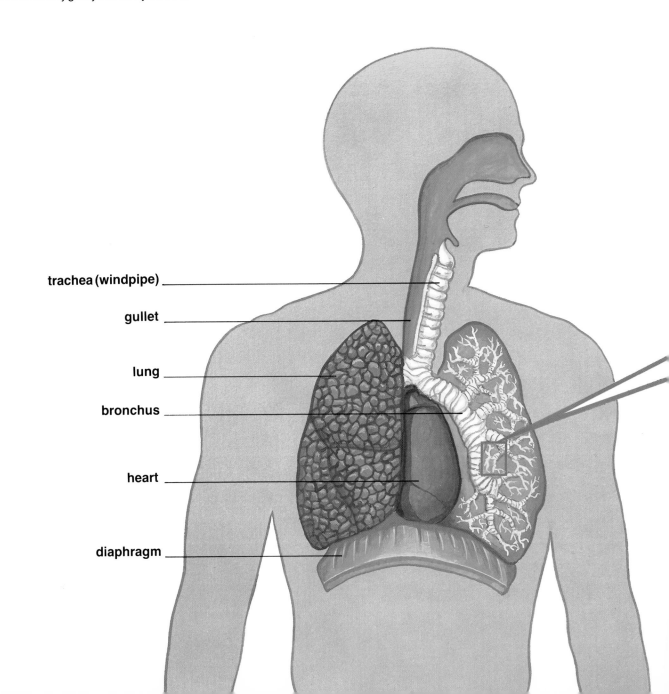

trachea (windpipe)

gullet

lung

bronchus

heart

diaphragm

Breathing in

You inhale air through your nose and mouth. Inside your nose are tiny hairs that catch dust from the air. There is also a sticky liquid called **mucus** that warms and moistens the incoming air and catches many of the germs you breathe in.

The air you breathe in goes down a pipe called the **trachea,** also known as your windpipe. From your windpipe, air enters each lung through two tubes called **bronchi.** Each bronchus divides into smaller and smaller tubes, which eventually lead to tiny, elastic sacs called **alveoli.** There are many millions of alveoli in each lung. When air enters the alveoli, they blow up like tiny balloons. Then oxygen from the air passes through the walls of the alveoli into **capillaries,** which are very tiny tubelike vessels through which blood flows.

Breathing out

At the same time as oxygen enters your blood, a waste gas passes from the blood into the alveoli. The air you exhale contains less oxygen and more carbon dioxide. This is the waste gas your body produces as oxygen breaks apart the chemicals in your food.

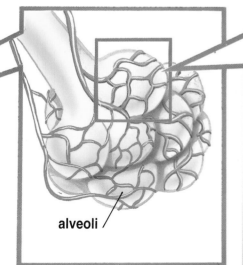

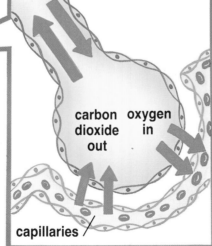

carbon dioxide out   oxygen in

When you breathe in, the alveoli in your lungs blow up like tiny balloons.

Oxygen passes into your capillaries. At the same time, carbon dioxide is passed out.

How you breathe

You have muscles in your chest that make you breathe. Some are fixed to your ribs and make your rib cage move in and out. Below your lungs is a strong, flat sheet of muscle called the **diaphragm.**

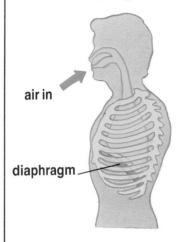

air in

diaphragm

As you breathe in, your diaphragm moves downwards and your rib cage moves out, or expands. This makes a bigger space for the air that enters your lungs.

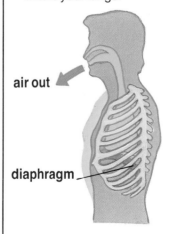

air out

diaphragm

As you breathe out, your rib cage and diaphragm squeeze your lungs into a smaller space again.

Around and around

Your blood has lots of different jobs to do as it travels around your body. It carries the oxygen you have breathed in to every single cell. It also carries food and other substances that your cells need. When the cells have done their job, they make waste products which your blood carries away.

What is blood made of ?

Like other parts of your body, your blood is made from cells. There are two main kinds of blood cells—red and white. The **red blood cells** are the ones that contain a red substance called **hemoglobin.** It is the hemoglobin in the red blood cells that carries oxygen from the lungs. The **white blood cells** kill germs that enter your body. There are fewer white cells than red cells.

A liquid called **plasma** surrounds the blood cells. This is made mostly of water. The plasma carries food to the cells and carries waste products away.

The tubes that carry blood

Blood travels through tubes called **blood vessels.** The vessels that carry oxygen-rich blood away from your heart are called **arteries.** The vessels that return the blood to your heart are called **veins.** There are thousands of arteries and veins all over your body. They branch into a network of very tiny, tubelike blood vessels called capillaries. These are very thin so that they can carry blood to all the cells of your body.

Inside your veins are tiny flaps called **valves.** These open as blood is pushed through after each heartbeat, and they close again to stop the blood from running backwards.

These blood cells came from human blood. The two white blood cells in the middle help to fight germs.

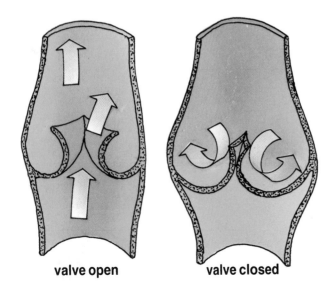

valve open   **valve closed**

The valve opens as the blood flows through. The valve then closes to keep the blood from flowing back.

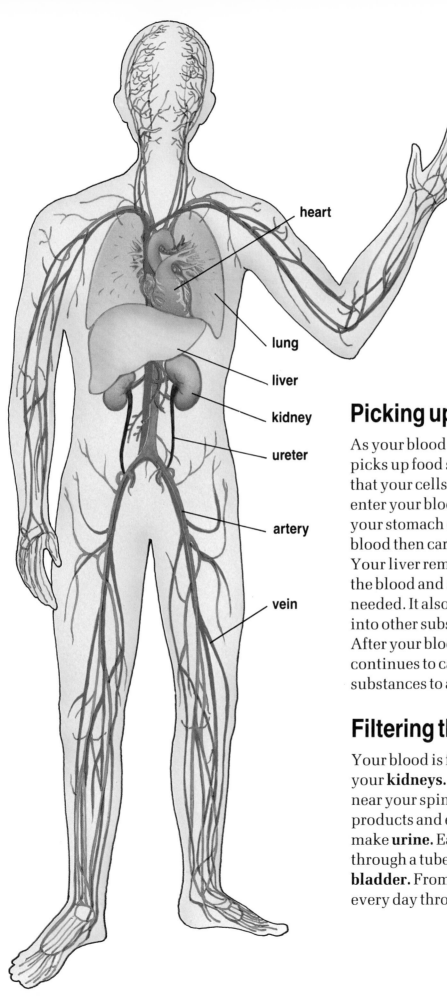

heart

lung

liver

kidney

ureter

artery

vein

Find out more by looking at
pages **20–21**
24–25

*Your heart is a strong muscle. It
pumps blood to all the different
parts of your body.*

Picking up food

As your blood flows through your body, it
picks up food substances, called **nutrients,**
that your cells need. Most of the nutrients
enter your bloodstream from an organ below
your stomach called the **small intestine.** Your
blood then carries the nutrients to your **liver.**
Your liver removes some of the nutrients from
the blood and stores them until they are
needed. It also changes some of the nutrients
into other substances that your body uses.
After your blood passes through your liver, it
continues to carry these nutrients and other
substances to all the cells.

Filtering the blood

Your blood is filtered when it passes through
your **kidneys.** These lie behind your stomach,
near your spine. They filter out some waste
products and extra salts from your blood and
make **urine.** Each kidney passes urine
through a tube, called a **ureter,** to your
bladder. From the bladder, you excrete urine
every day through the **urethra.**

Find out more by looking at
pages **16–17**
18–19

Your heart

Your heart acts like a pump that's always working. It's made of strong muscle and is about the size of your fist. As it beats, it pumps blood to all the different parts of your body.

Blood from your heart carries oxygen that you breathe into your lungs to all the millions of cells in your body. Your body cells need oxygen to carry out their work and keep you alive.

How does your heart work?

Your heart has two main pumping parts that have different jobs to do. The left part pumps blood very strongly through the arteries of your body. This blood contains fresh oxygen from your lungs. The right part of your heart takes in blood returning from the veins of your body. This blood contains carbon dioxide, which is the waste gas that your cells give out as they use up oxygen. This blood is then pumped to your lungs, where carbon dioxide is exchanged for oxygen. The blood containing this fresh oxygen then continues to flow into the left part of your heart, from where it is pumped around your body once again.

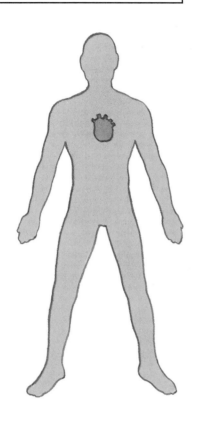

Your heart lies in your chest cavity, a little to the left of center.

Valves in each part of your heart open and shut in a way that prevents blood from flowing backwards.

Faster and slower

After you have been running, your heart beats faster and you breathe more quickly. Why does this happen? The amount of carbon dioxide in your blood increases when you have been exercising. The rate and depth of your breathing increase to take the carbon dioxide out of your body. At the same time, the amount of oxygen you take in is increased.

artery

to lungs

to body

from body

from lungs

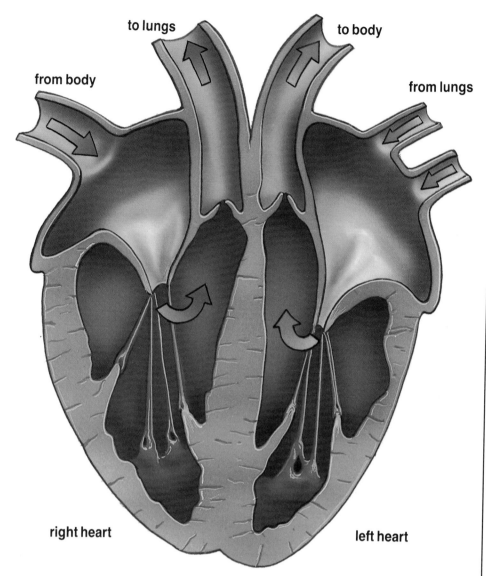

right heart

left heart

Speed up your pulse

1. Using a watch or clock with a second hand, count how many times your pulse beats in 30 seconds. Double the result to get your heart rate.

2. Then do some kind of exercise, such as skipping, for a few minutes.

3. Count your pulse beats again. How many are there in 30 seconds now? What is your heart rate?

Your **pulse** shows how fast your heart is beating. Every time your heart beats, blood surges through the artery in your wrist. If you put two fingers of one hand on the wrist of your other hand, you should feel a gentle and regular throbbing. This is your pulse. Use two fingers as shown.

You can feel your pulse at any point where an artery is near the surface of your skin.

Find out more by looking at page **60**

Where does your food go?

When you eat, your food begins a long journey through your body. Most of your food is broken down into lots of tiny, simple pieces so that your body can use it. This breaking-down process starts in your mouth and is called **digestion.** The various substances that aid in digestion are known as **digestive juices.**

Your body uses food to acquire energy. Food contains special chemicals that provide energy in your body's cells. Energy keeps all the different parts of your body working. Without energy, all your muscles and every other part of you would stop working. Food also helps your body grow and repair parts that have become worn out or damaged.

Food to keep you healthy

Food contains many different substances that work together to keep you going. Food substances that give you energy are called **carbohydrates** and **fats.** Carbohydrates are found in foods like potatoes, rice, and bread. Milk, butter, and cheese are fatty foods. The parts of your food that help your body grow and mend itself are called **proteins.** These are mainly found in meat, milk, eggs, nuts, and grain.

Your food also contains **vitamins** and **minerals,** which help you stay healthy. They make the chemicals in your body work properly. Food also contains tough parts called **fiber.** Fiber helps to keep your intestines in good working order. We take in water from our food, as well as water from what we drink. Your blood needs a great deal of water to carry all these substances around your body.

2. After you have swallowed the food, it passes into your stomach, where a strong acid breaks it down. This process is helped by special chemicals called **enzymes.** There are lots of muscles in the stomach wall that mix the food up with digestive juices. The stomach acid also helps to kill germs in your food.

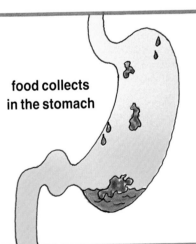

food collects in the stomach

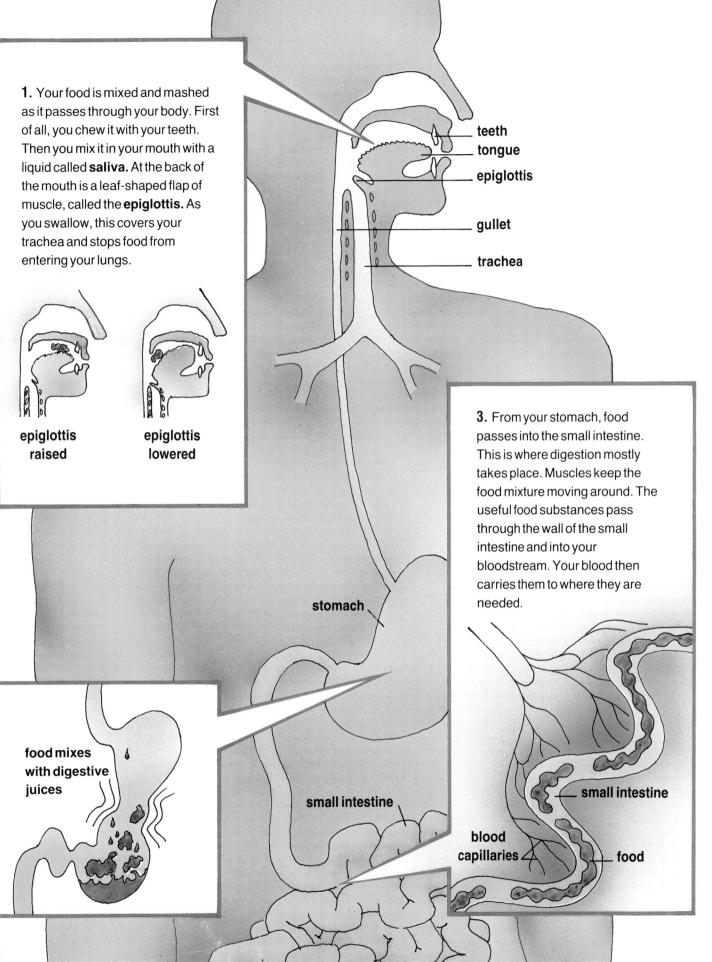

1. Your food is mixed and mashed as it passes through your body. First of all, you chew it with your teeth. Then you mix it in your mouth with a liquid called **saliva.** At the back of the mouth is a leaf-shaped flap of muscle, called the **epiglottis.** As you swallow, this covers your trachea and stops food from entering your lungs.

epiglottis raised

epiglottis lowered

teeth

tongue

epiglottis

gullet

trachea

3. From your stomach, food passes into the small intestine. This is where digestion mostly takes place. Muscles keep the food mixture moving around. The useful food substances pass through the wall of the small intestine and into your bloodstream. Your blood then carries them to where they are needed.

stomach

food mixes with digestive juices

small intestine

small intestine

blood capillaries

food

Find out more by looking at pages **18–19**

Clearing away waste

To keep you healthy, your body clears away the waste materials it cannot use. You breathe out a waste gas called carbon dioxide from your lungs. Your body can't digest some food, such as tough plant fibres. So you get rid of them as solid waste. Your body gets rid of other substances as liquid waste.

Getting rid of solid waste

Below the small intestine is the **large intestine.** Most of the food that reaches the large intestine is waste food. The large intestine takes in, or absorbs, most of the water and minerals from the food as the food travels through it. This leaves solid waste, called **feces,** which collects in the lower bowel, or intestine, before it passes out from your body through an opening called the **anus.**

What are your kidneys?

Your kidneys make the waste liquid your body has to get rid of. You have two kidneys, one on each side of your spine, behind your stomach. They are shaped like beans and are nearly as large as your heart.

Your kidneys filter your blood as it travels through them. They take out waste products that your blood has carried away from all the cells. One of the main waste products is called **urea.** This is made after your cells have broken down substances called proteins. Your kidneys also take away some salt and water from your blood if it contains too much of them. Your body must keep a balance of salt and water. Keeping this balance is the responsibility of the kidneys.

Your kidneys then get rid of the water and waste products by making droplets of a liquid called urine. The urine passes into your bladder through two tubes called ureters. Your bladder is a bag made of muscle, which stretches as it fills with urine. When you decide it's time to expel the urine, the bladder squeezes it out through a tube called the urethra.

Your lungs remove carbon dioxide from your blood. Your kidneys remove waste liquid as urine, and your anus removes waste solids as feces.

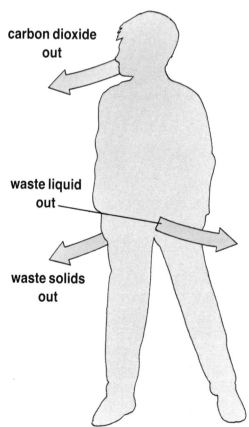

carbon dioxide out

waste liquid out

waste solids out

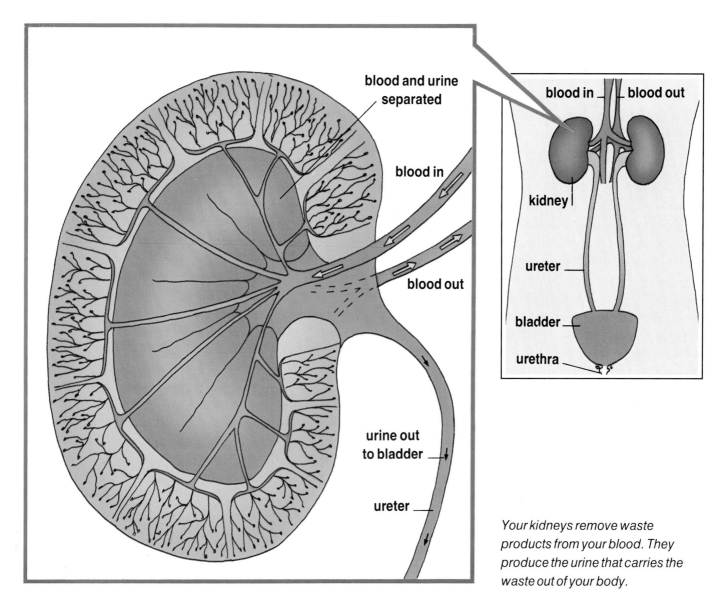

blood and urine separated

blood in

blood out

urine out to bladder

ureter

blood in | blood out

kidney

ureter

bladder

urethra

Your kidneys remove waste products from your blood. They produce the urine that carries the waste out of your body.

Kidney machines

If your kidneys stop working properly, dangerous waste products stay in your blood. A **kidney machine** can filter your blood in the same way as a real kidney. Blood from the patient's body is pumped through a filter in the machine. The filter takes out the waste products. A second pump returns blood back to the patient.

filter

pump

pump

blood in

blood out

Your senses

Can you name the "five senses"? Try to name them before reading further.

These senses send information to the brain. There are special parts in the brain that sort out this information. It is then passed to other parts of the brain, which can compare information from different sense organs. Your brain then signals what you are seeing, hearing, smelling, tasting, and touching. These five senses allow you to know what is in your physical environment.

Sense organs are specially developed parts of your body. For example, each of your eyes has a retina for detecting light. And each of your ears has a cochlea for detecting sounds.

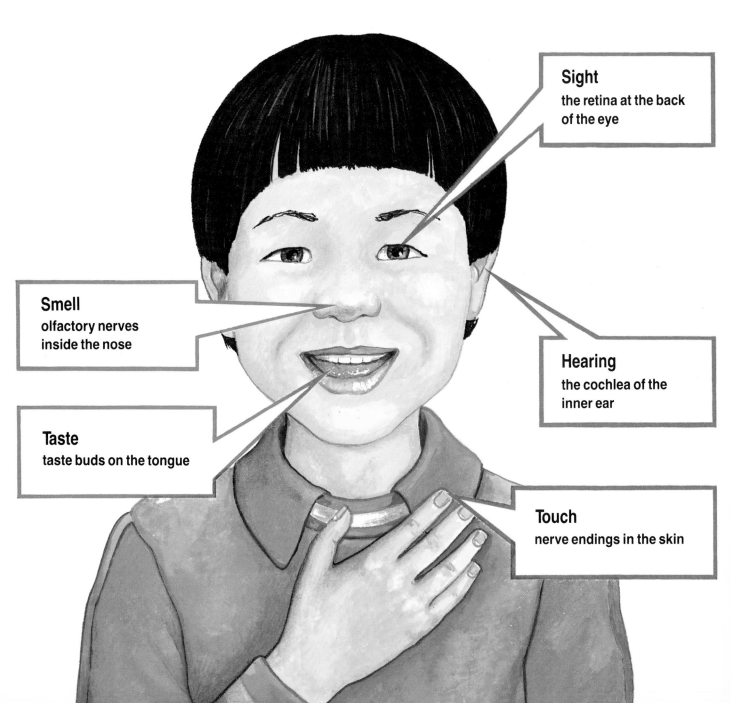

Sight
the retina at the back of the eye

Smell
olfactory nerves inside the nose

Hearing
the cochlea of the inner ear

Taste
taste buds on the tongue

Touch
nerve endings in the skin

The hidden senses

Another set of senses, of which you are unaware of most of the time, helps control your inner organs. These senses control the timing and movement of food through your body. They measure the amount of sugar and salt in your blood. They regulate the amount of oxygen that's taken in. Your body temperature and the fullness of your bladder are also under the control of these senses. Without your awareness, your body is always receiving messages from your hidden senses. They keep all these basic processes, such as breathing and digestion, running smoothly.

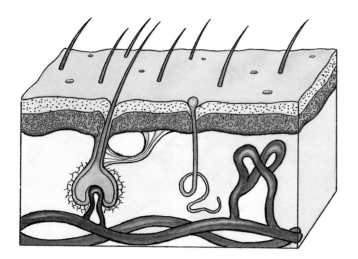

When you're hot, your skin produces droplets of sweat.

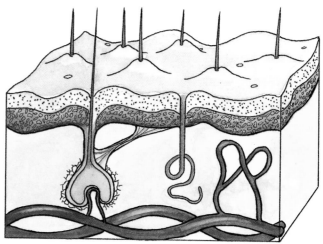

When you're cold, the hairs on your skin stand on end.

A sense of time

Are you always late for everything? Or do you have a good "sense of time"? In fact, we all have a sense of time, often called our **biological clock.** It is something that we have in common with almost all animals. No one knows for certain what it is or how it works, but you are somehow aware when day changes into night, and night into day. During experiments, scientists have lived in deep, dark caves for periods of time. They found that, despite the darkness, their biological clock woke them up in the morning and made them slow down at night.

How do you hear?

Your ears are organs. They aren't just the flaps of skin you can see! Your ears stretch deep into the skull. They do a very important job. They collect sound waves, which are tiny vibrations of air, and change them into signals that your brain can understand.

To do the difficult job of hearing, the ear has three different parts. These are called the **outer ear,** the **middle ear,** and the **inner ear.**

The outer ear

The outer ear consists of the ear flap, which is the part you can see, and a hollow tube, called the **ear canal.** This leads to the **eardrum.** The eardrum is made of a sheet of skinlike material called a **membrane.** This vibrates when sound waves travel down the ear canal.

The middle ear

The middle ear is like a hollow cave. It contains three bones, called the **hammer,** the **anvil,** and the **stirrup.** When the eardrum vibrates, it makes the hammer vibrate. This movement is passed on to the anvil and then to the stirrup. The stirrup makes another membrane, called the **oval window,** vibrate.

The inner ear

Behind the oval window is the inner ear. This is made up of the **cochlea,** the **vestibule,** and the **semicircular canals.** The cochlea has three tubes, which are coiled like a snail's shell. These tubes are filled with fluid. When the oval window vibrates, it makes waves in the fluid. One of the tubes has thousands of sensitive hairs. When the fluid passes over the hairs, it prompts your nerves to carry messages about sound to your brain.

An acrobat needs to have a very good sense of balance to do a trick like this.

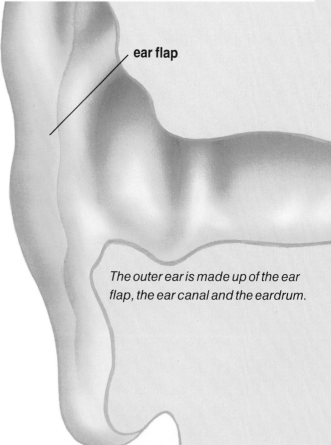

ear flap

The outer ear is made up of the ear flap, the ear canal and the eardrum.

Keeping your balance

The semicircular canals help you keep your balance. They also contain fluid and sensitive hairs. If you tip your head to one side, the fluid in these tubes moves, and the sensitive hairs let the brain know what has happened.

The vestibule is a chamber between the canals and the cochlea. It contains two sacs, also filled with fluid and sensitive hair cells. The sacs have chalky particles inside them, which are pulled to the earth by the force of gravity. When you stand upright, the particles press on the hairs at the bottom of each sac. When you lie down, the particles settle to one side and press on a different set of hairs. Nerves from the hairs signal your brain about the position of your body.

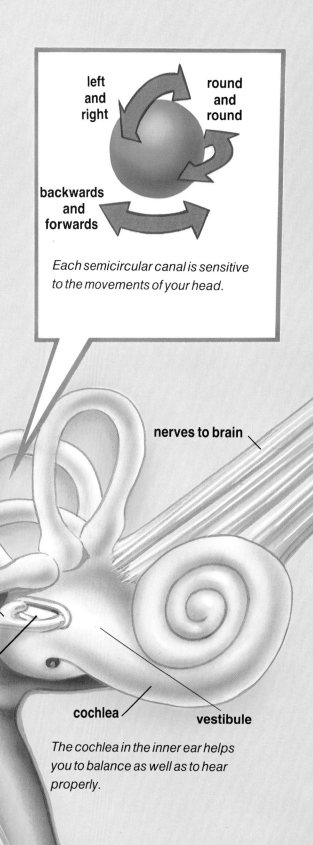

left and right

round and round

backwards and forwards

Each semicircular canal is sensitive to the movements of your head.

semicircular canals

stirrup

anvil

hammer

nerves to brain

ear canal

eardrum

oval window

cochlea

vestibule

tube to throat

The middle ear contains three tiny bones — the hammer, the anvil and the stirrup.

The cochlea in the inner ear helps you to balance as well as to hear properly.

Taste and smell

Your tongue is your main taste organ. You also use your tongue to break up and swallow your food. Your tongue is covered with tiny spots called **taste buds.** They allow you to notice the difference between the four tastes—**sweet, salty, sour,** and **bitter.**

You will need:

five sheets of paper

a pencil

water

sugar

salt

vinegar or lemon juice

strong, unsweetened black tea or coffee

paper tissues

four saucers

4 glass or plastic droppers, or 4 small teaspoons

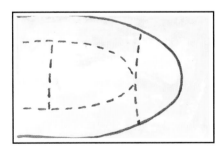

6. Now you are ready to map a tongue! Ask a friend to stick his or her tongue out. Copy its outline on a sheet of paper.

7. Now divide the tongue up into five areas as pictured above.

Map your tongue

There are four areas on your tongue which pick up different tastes. Find them by making a map of the tongue.

1. First, label four of the sheets of paper as "sweet," "salty," "sour," and "bitter."

2. In one saucer, dissolve some sugar in water. Place this saucer on the paper marked "sweet."

3. In another saucer, dissolve some salt in water. Place this on the paper marked "salty."

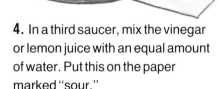

4. In a third saucer, mix the vinegar or lemon juice with an equal amount of water. Put this on the paper marked "sour."

5. Pour the tea into the last saucer. Place this on the paper marked "bitter."

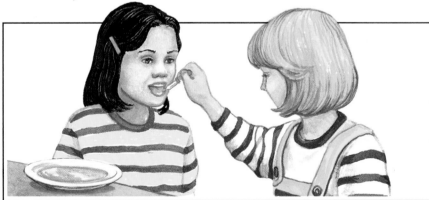

8. Wash your hands well. Dry your friend's tongue with a paper tissue and place a drop of the sweet liquid on the tip of the tongue. If your friend can taste the sweetness, mark that part of your map "sweet." Do the same for the other three liquids, using a new dropper or spoon for each type.

9. Now do the same for the other four areas of the tongue, but test the liquids in a different order each time.

What does your tongue map show? Does each area of the tongue pick up a different taste?

A sense of smell

Smells are really chemicals floating about in the air. Your nose has special parts called **receptors** that respond to these smells. If a chemical appears, a receptor sends a message along the nerves to your brain. Your brain translates this message into a sensation of a "nice" or a "nasty" smell. Your nose is sensitive to different kinds of chemicals, but it can't interpret them.

Smell is important to us because it helps our sense of taste. Your tongue can only pick up the four basic tastes — sweet, salty, sour, and bitter. It's your nose that makes tomatoes taste like tomatoes and apples taste like apples. Without a sense of smell, they would taste much the same.

Find out more by looking at pages **40–41**

You will need:

a knife

a blindfold

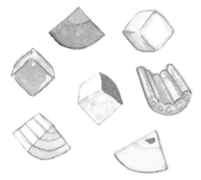

some foods, such as apple, celery, melon, potato, carrot, and onion

Hold your nose!

You can test the sense of smell by feeding different foods to a friend who is blindfolded while holding his or her nose. All the foods should have about the same texture.

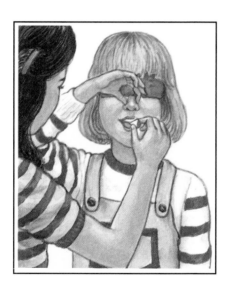

1. Wash your hands well with soap and water. Then cut up the foods into pieces. Blindfold your friend and make sure your friend is holding his or her nose.

2. Now feed each of these foods in turn to your friend. Give the onion last. Otherwise its strong taste might spoil the other tastes. Can your friend tell you what the different foods are?

3. Now ask your friend to try each food again, but hold another type of food under your friend's nose at the same time. What happens?

Find out more by looking at pages **40–41**

Your outer covering

Your skin protects your body. It keeps out dirt, rain, and wind. It also has many other jobs to do. In your skin, there are nerves that sense pain, temperature, and pressure. These nerves act as sensors and send messages to your brain. They give you your sense of touch.

Touching gives you different kinds of sensations. Close your eyes and run your fingers over some objects around you. Describe what your fingertips are feeling.

You will need:

hot water

cold water

three glass jars

Hot and cold

Does your body feel temperature changes as accurately as a thermometer? Find out by following this experiment.

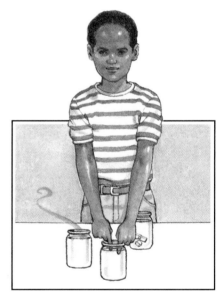

1. Fill one jar with hot tap water, not too hot to put your finger in. Fill the other jar with cold water, or iced water if available. In the third jar, make a mixture of the two.

Remember that even hot tap water can scald!

2. Place the forefinger of one hand into the jar of hot water and the forefinger of your other hand into the jar of cold water. Leave them there for a few minutes.

3. Now take both fingers out, and immediately put them into the third jar. What are your fingers telling you about the temperature of the water? Are they saying the same thing?

Your skin does not measure temperature as accurately as a thermometer, does it? Your estimation of temperature depends on how hot or cold your skin is to begin with.

Beneath your skin

The skin on your body has three layers. The top layer is called the **epidermis.** It contains four layers of cells. The next layer of skin is called the **dermis.** Your nerves are found here. It also contains small tissues called **glands.** These produce a liquid called **sweat** and another substance which oils the hairs and skin. The **fatty layer** is the deepest layer. In all people it varies in thickness.

Sweating it out

When we get too hot, our bodies are in danger. Many parts of our bodies will work properly only if the temperature inside is just right—about 98.6 °F (37 °C). In particular, the vital chemicals called **enzymes** are of no use if the temperature is too high or too low. Some way of cooling high body temperature is necessary to maintain a fairly constant temperature.

The main way that we cool down is by producing sweat. This liquid oozes out of the **pores** in our skin whenever the body temperature is too high. When this liquid evaporates, it takes away heat, causing the body to "cool down." **Evaporation** of sweat from the skin's surface is thus a cooling process.

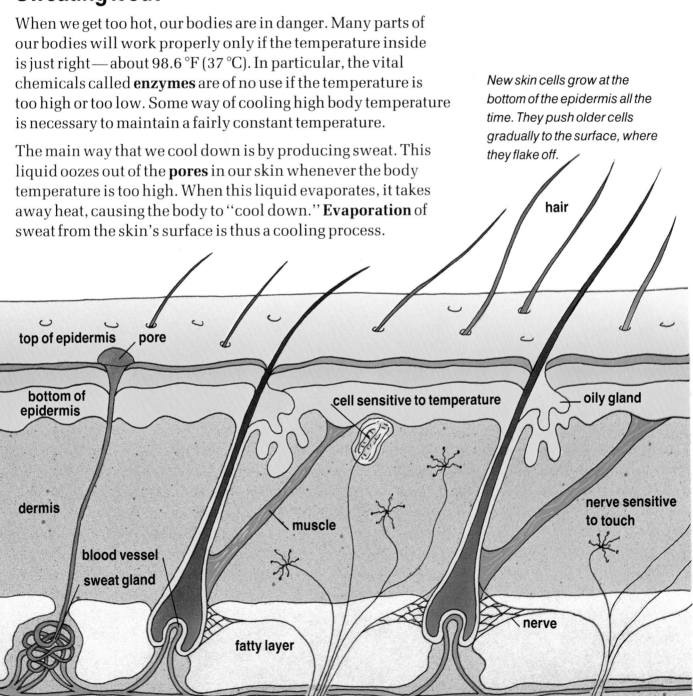

New skin cells grow at the bottom of the epidermis all the time. They push older cells gradually to the surface, where they flake off.

hair

top of epidermis   pore

bottom of epidermis

cell sensitive to temperature   oily gland

dermis

muscle

nerve sensitive to touch

blood vessel

sweat gland

nerve

fatty layer

The amazing eye

Your eyes are like two tiny movie cameras inside your head. They are sending a steady stream of pictures back to your brain, like a television camera sending live pictures back to a TV screen.

Your eyes have a part called the **lens,** just like a camera. The lens helps to bring everything you look at into focus, so that details are as clear as possible.

The colored ring in your eye is a band of muscle called the **iris.**

The outer eye is covered by a transparent tissue called the **cornea.** The cornea focuses light through the pupil.

The **pupil** looks like a black circle, but it is a hole in a ring of muscle. The pupil opens up to let in more light at night and closes up on bright, sunny days.

Light travels through your pupil to the **retina** at the back of your eye. The retina contains special cells, called rods and cones, which respond to light and color. Nerves carry messages from these cells to your brain.

Rods and cones

Human beings are luckier than many other animals because they see in color. Some other animals, such as birds and butterflies, can also see colors.

To see colors, we have special cells in the eye called **cones.** They share the work of seeing with other cells called **rods.** Rods do not detect the difference between colors and don't need as much light as cones to make them work. So at times, rods are more useful to you than cones, such as at night when the light is very dim.

Have you ever been for a walk in the moonlight and noticed how pale, silvery, and colorless everything seems? Photographers can take pictures by moonlight which are just as colorful as pictures taken by day. So the colors are still there by moonlight, but we can't see them. Can you think why this is?

The cones help us to see color, but moonlight doesn't provide them with enough light to function well at night.

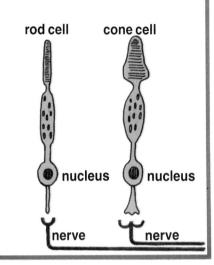

The rods and cones in your retina absorb the light which enters your eye. They pass messages about the light through nerves to your brain.

rod cell   cone cell

nucleus   nucleus

nerve   nerve

Changing shape

Muscles pull on the lens to change its shape. This allows you to look at something far away and then to focus on an object close by. As you look from the far-away object to the nearby one, your lens changes shape. A sharp picture of the object is focused onto the back of the inside of your eyeball. When you look back at the far-away scene, the lens changes back to its original shape so quickly that you don't even notice.

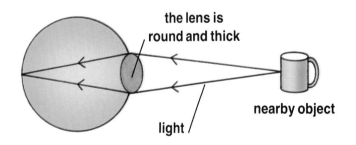

the lens is
round and thick

nearby object

light

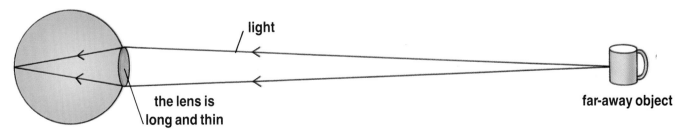

light

the lens is
long and thin

far-away object

Find out more by looking at pages **34—35**

Different animals have their eyes in different positions on their head.

Why do we have two eyes?

Look at the pictures of the woodcock and the boy on this page. What do you notice about the position of their eyes?

Why do you think the woodcock has its eyes on the sides of its head? If you watch a woodcock feeding, you will see why. The woodcock has to keep a constant lookout for enemies such as foxes, so it needs to be able to see all around. In fact, many birds can see all around them, to help protect them from danger.

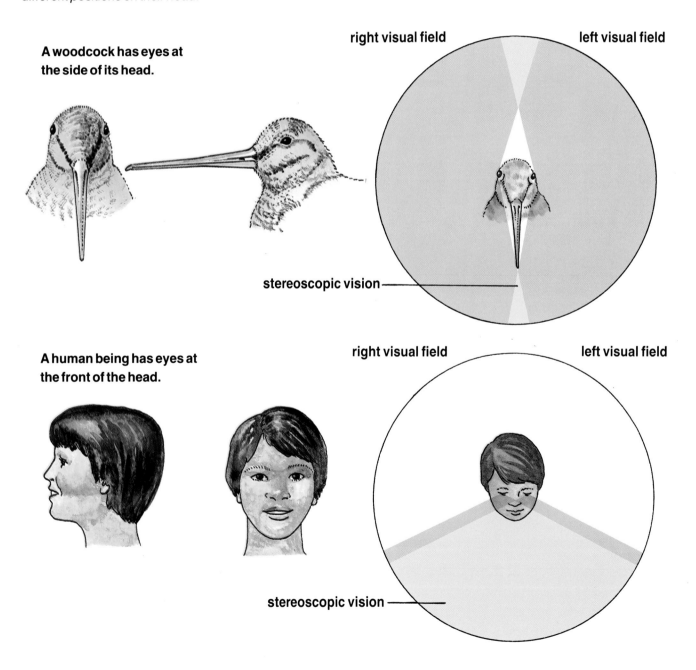

A woodcock has eyes at the side of its head.

right visual field left visual field

stereoscopic vision

A human being has eyes at the front of the head.

right visual field left visual field

stereoscopic vision

You will need:

stiff, black paper or cloth

scissors

a sharp pencil

a ball

thin elastic or ribbon

Two eyes are better than one

Why are our eyes on the front of our head, both looking the same way? It seems a waste of an eye, doesn't it? To discover the answer, play this game of throwing and catching a ball with a friend.

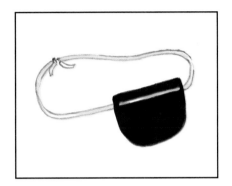

1. Cut out an eyepatch from the paper or cloth. Using the pencil point, make a small hole on either side of the patch. Thread the elastic or ribbon through the patch.

2. Play at catching the ball with both eyes first. Throw the ball 20 times, and make a record of how often you drop the ball.

3. Now cover one eye with your patch. Keep a record for another 20 catches. Did you do as well? Explain what happened.

Stereoscopic vision

When we use both our eyes, we have a kind of sight called **stereoscopic vision.** Because both eyes are at the front, they both see the same object. But your eyes are a little apart from each other, so each has a slightly different view of things. You can check this if you place two objects, such as drinking glasses, on a table in front of you. Place one about 8 inches (20 centimeters) away from you, the other 2 feet (60 centimeters) away. Put your chin on the table with the two glasses in a straight line away from you. Close one eye, then the other. Do you see exactly the same thing with both eyes?

Your brain makes use of the fact that your eyes tell different stories. By comparing the messages from each eye, your brain works out how far away an object is. Your brain does this in a split second every time you look at anything.

Find out more by looking at pages **36 – 37**

Children may take several years to develop good coordination. They learn to coordinate their hands and eyes when doing simple things, such as balancing blocks on top of one another.

Coordinating your body

Your brain is a most remarkable organ! It sends out and receives hundreds of messages every second of your life. Your brain controls your muscles, sense organs, temperature— even your appetite! Your brain is also the place where thinking and remembering happen.

Your brain plays a very important part in your body's **coordination.** It controls the messages from your muscles and sense organs. When you stand on your toes, your brain receives messages from your eyes, ears, and joints about the position of your body. At the same time, your brain signals to your muscles what to do to keep your body balanced.

Is seeing always believing?

All you need for this experiment is a narrow cardboard tube or a sheet of paper rolled up to make a tube.

1. Look out of the window and hold the tube to your right eye. Close your left eye to check what your right eye is seeing.

Now open both eyes. What can you see? Explain what happens.

2. Still with both eyes open, hold your left hand up in front of you, your open palm toward your face. Lightly touching the tube with the side of your hand, slowly slide your hand back and forth until you see a hole in the middle of the palm. What can you see through the hole?

3. Still holding the tube to your eye, hold a finger up next to the tube. Is there a hole in your finger? Can you explain the difference?

Your brain sorts it out

When you held up your hand, the part of your brain that receives information from your eyes became confused. It had to match up two completely different views coming from your eyes. It matched these views by showing your hand with a hole in the middle that framed the view through the tube. When you were just holding up a finger, it could sort out the two views because the finger did not blot out the view through the tube completely. So it did not need to make a hole in the finger.

This experiment shows you something even more important about your brain. You never thought that your hand really had a hole in it. Another part of your brain told you that information from your eyes was incorrect. So your brain has a special part that makes sense of confusing information.

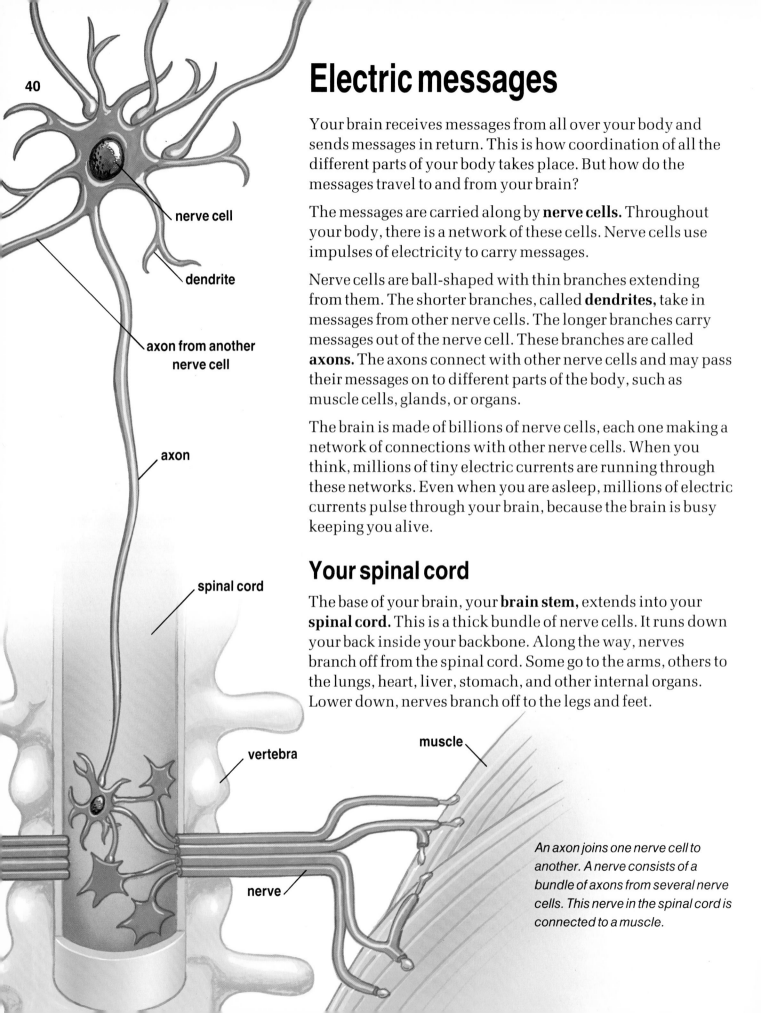

nerve cell

dendrite

axon from another
nerve cell

axon

spinal cord

vertebra

nerve

muscle

Electric messages

Your brain receives messages from all over your body and sends messages in return. This is how coordination of all the different parts of your body takes place. But how do the messages travel to and from your brain?

The messages are carried along by **nerve cells.** Throughout your body, there is a network of these cells. Nerve cells use impulses of electricity to carry messages.

Nerve cells are ball-shaped with thin branches extending from them. The shorter branches, called **dendrites,** take in messages from other nerve cells. The longer branches carry messages out of the nerve cell. These branches are called **axons.** The axons connect with other nerve cells and may pass their messages on to different parts of the body, such as muscle cells, glands, or organs.

The brain is made of billions of nerve cells, each one making a network of connections with other nerve cells. When you think, millions of tiny electric currents are running through these networks. Even when you are asleep, millions of electric currents pulse through your brain, because the brain is busy keeping you alive.

Your spinal cord

The base of your brain, your **brain stem,** extends into your **spinal cord.** This is a thick bundle of nerve cells. It runs down your back inside your backbone. Along the way, nerves branch off from the spinal cord. Some go to the arms, others to the lungs, heart, liver, stomach, and other internal organs. Lower down, nerves branch off to the legs and feet.

An axon joins one nerve cell to another. A nerve consists of a bundle of axons from several nerve cells. This nerve in the spinal cord is connected to a muscle.

Reflex movements

Your leg muscles flex and move to allow you to stand up because your brain has sent them messages on what to do. But there are some movements, such as drawing your hand away from something hot, which do not involve the brain. These are called **reflexes.** Reflexes help to protect you from danger. Blinking your eyes as something comes very near to your face is another reflex.

Doctors can test whether your reflexes are working properly by using the knee-jerk test. You sit on a chair with one leg crossed over the other. The doctor taps a spot just below the knee of the top leg, and your leg jerks into the air. You can't control it. When your knee is tapped, a message travels up a nerve in your thigh to your spinal cord. It does not go to the brain. The spinal cord sends a message straight back to a nerve connected to the thigh muscle. This muscle contracts suddenly and your leg jerks upwards.

Find out more by looking at pages **34–35**
38–39

41

It takes a very short time for the knee-jerk message to travel to your spinal cord and back to your muscle —only about one-twentieth of a second.

doctor taps your knee here

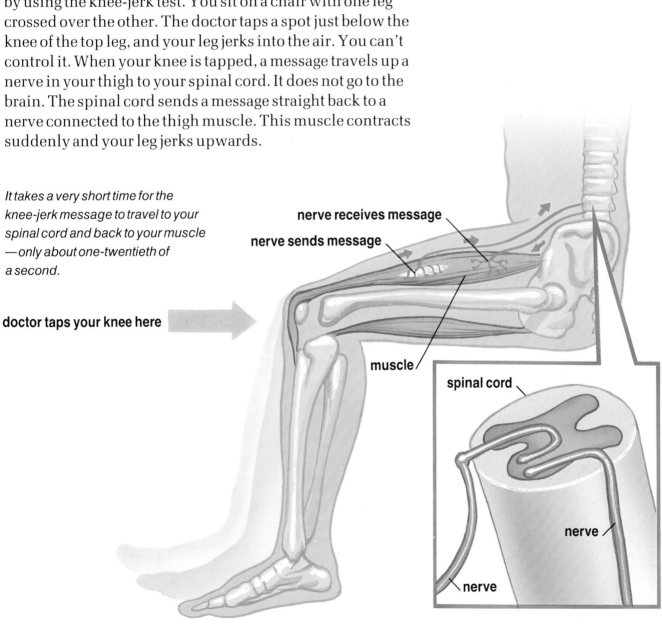

nerve receives message

nerve sends message

muscle

spinal cord

nerve

nerve

Controlling movement

You have discovered that your brain is responsible for coordinating many of your body's movements. These movements can be directly controlled by you — unlike reflexes which do not involve the brain. But these movements do not always come naturally — often they have to be learned. If you want to ride a bicycle, you must learn to pedal, to balance, and to lean to one side when you ride around a corner.

You will need:

a long ruler

paper

a felt-tipped pen

Test the speed of your reactions

In these tests, you can find out about the speed of your sense of sight and sense of touch. In both these tests, hold your thumb and forefinger so that they are just touching the ruler. For the sight test, watch the ruler to see when it falls and grab it as quickly as possible. For the touch test, close your eyes and grab the ruler as soon as you feel it falling.

Do some sight tests and some touch tests. Then make separate record sheets for each test. Record the distances measured on the ruler for every test you do. Ask a friend to help you.

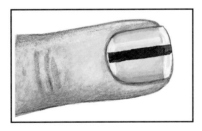

1. First, ask your friend to draw a line on your thumbnail with the pen. This is lined up with the line marked 'O' on the ruler each time the test is carried out.

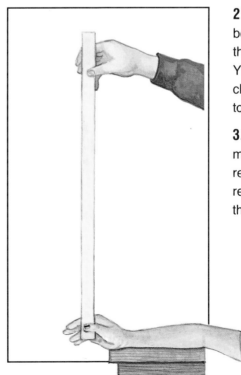

2. Ask your friend to hold the ruler between the thumb and forefinger, then to drop it without any warning. You must try to catch the ruler by closing your thumb and forefinger together as quickly as you can.

3. Use the lines on the ruler as a measure of how long it took you to react. Each time you catch the ruler, record the place where the thumbnail line is.

Which type of reaction is faster? What does this test show?

Learning actions

You can learn to make certain movements or actions by practicing them over and over again. When you get used to them, your brain helps you to do them almost automatically. Once a baby has learned to walk, for example, he or she will be able to walk without having to think about it. Though the act of walking is more or less automatic, the child can still choose to walk slowly or quickly.

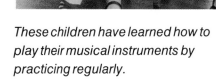

Practice makes perfect

Does a task you're not used to doing take longer than a task you are used to doing? Can you get better and quicker at the task by doing it again and again?

You will need:

three sheets of lined paper

a pencil

a watch with a second hand

These children have learned how to play their musical instruments by practicing regularly.

1. Number the lines on a sheet of paper from 1 to 20.

2. Time yourself as you write out any word 20 times. You can write your name if you like. At the bottom of the page, write down how long it took.

3. Number 20 lines on the second sheet of paper.

4. Timing yourself again, write the word 20 times backwards. How long did this take?

5. On the third sheet of paper, write out the word backwards another 20 times. Has your speed improved?

Chemicals in charge

Are you tall for your age, or short? How tall you grow depends mostly on chemical substances called **hormones,** which move around your body in your blood.

Some hormones cause the cells in your body to make more protein. They then make the cells grow and divide, so that all of your body gets bigger. Because hormones are going around in your blood, they reach every cell in your body. So all your cells grow and divide at your normal rate. Can you imagine how it would be if some parts of your body grew faster than others? This is why hormones are so important. They control the different parts of your body, so that everything is regulated. Hormones are regulators of chemical and growth activity in the body.

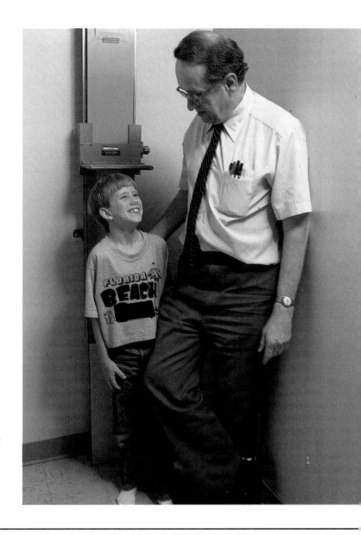

A special kind of hormone, called growth hormone, helps the long bones to grow. Children who do not produce enough of this hormone may not grow as tall as they would be able to grow with the hormone.

Linking with your brain

The balance of hormones in your blood is controlled by the **pituitary gland,** which lies just below the brain. The pituitary gland produces hormones which control many of the body's activities. Large numbers of nerve cells and blood vessels link the pituitary gland to a part of the brain called the **hypothalamus.** The hypothalamus controls the pituitary gland by sending "on" and "off" messages through the nerve cells and the bloodstream. These messages affect the pituitary gland with regard to the releasing of its hormones.

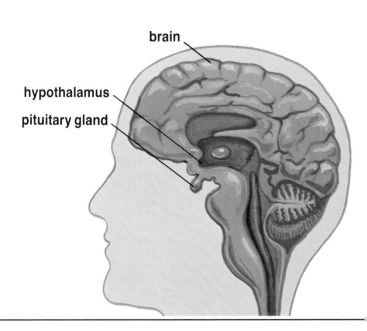

brain

hypothalamus

pituitary gland

Glands produce hormones

Most of your body's hormones are produced by **glands,** which are also known as **endocrine glands.** The hormones made by your pituitary gland control the production of hormones from some of the other glands.

The **pituitary gland** is the main hormone-producing gland. It lies just underneath your brain. The pituitary gland produces many different hormones, like the ones that control your growth and others that control your kidneys.

The **thyroid gland** lies in your neck, on either side of your trachea. It produces hormones which make your body processes go faster or slower.

The **adrenal glands** lie just above your kidneys. They produce hormones that control the amount of salts and **glucose** (a type of sugar) in your blood. They also produce **adrenalin,** which prepares your body for danger.

The **pancreas** produces the hormone **insulin,** which controls the amount of sugar in your blood. Its juices help you to digest your food.

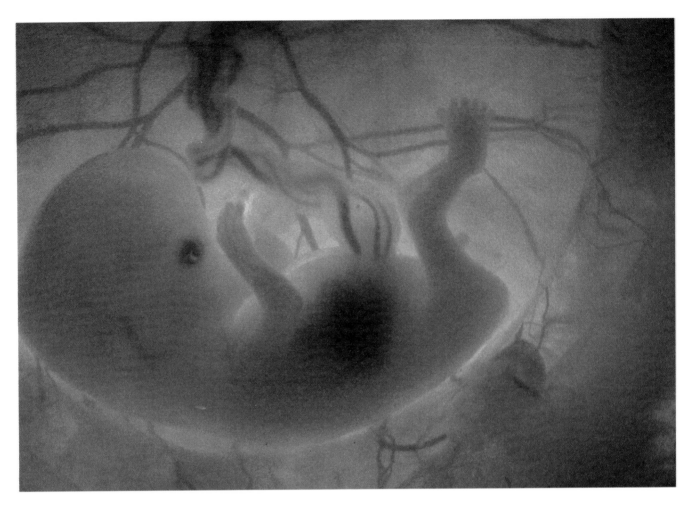

This fetus is 12 weeks old.

This fetus is 38 weeks old. The baby will soon be born.

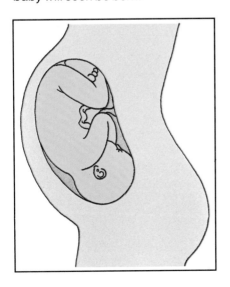

Where and how you began life

If you were a bird or a fish, you would have begun life by hatching out of an egg. Because you belong to a group of animals called mammals, you spent the first nine months of your life inside your mother. Human beings produce eggs, just as birds and fish do, but they are much smaller than the head of a pin. The mother keeps the fertilized egg inside her, so that her baby can grow protected from the outside world. Before the baby is born, it's called a **fetus.** The fetus grows inside a part of the mother called the **uterus,** or womb.

While you were growing inside your mother, you took in nourishment through a flexible tube called the **umbilical cord.** This was joined to a disk-shaped organ inside the uterus called the **placenta.** As your mother's blood flowed through the placenta, it supplied you with all the food and oxygen you needed.

Growing inside the womb

For nine months, you grew larger and slowly changed shape inside your mother's womb. Then the time came when you were ready to be born.

A mother carries the baby inside her body for nine months. During this period, the fetus grows and develops until it is ready to be born.

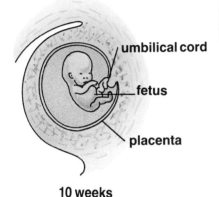

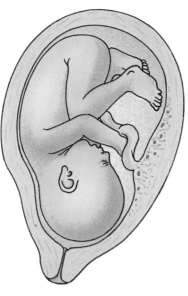

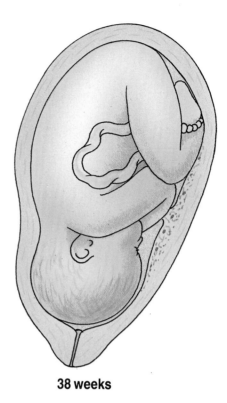

10 weeks

22 weeks

38 weeks

Being born

During your birth, strong muscles in your mother's womb squeezed you out into a passage called the **vagina.** From here, you came out into the world. Then the umbilical cord, which attached you to the placenta, was cut. Your belly button, called the **navel,** is where the cord was once attached to you. After you were born you continued to grow. Your body grows rapidly until you are between the ages of 12 and 17, then continues to grow more slowly until you reach your adult size by about the age of 23.

During birth, muscles inside the mother's womb push the baby out through the vagina.

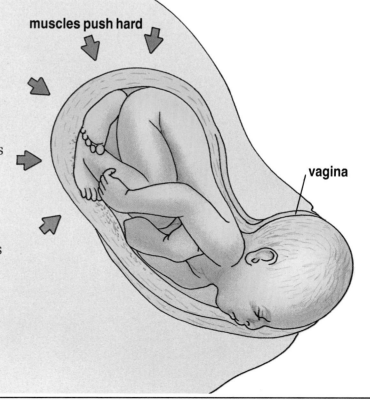

muscles push hard

vagina

Find out more by looking at
pages **52–53**
        56–57

What makes you ill?

You can get sick in various ways—from not eating a balanced diet to breathing in too many automobile fumes. You can also become ill by catching a disease. Many diseases are caused by small living things, such as **bacteria** and **viruses,** which can live inside your body. Often we call these things germs, but scientists call them **microorganisms,** or **microbes.** The microbes are always trying to attack you, and your body has to fight to stop them, or it becomes ill. Other living things called **protists** can cause disease, too. Larger creatures, such as worms and flukes, can also live inside people and make them ill.

These rod-shaped bacteria are on a human tooth. They are not really red but have been colored so that they are easier to see.

Bacteria

Bacteria are so small that you can see them only through a microscope. Some bacteria cause diseases such as scarlet fever, salmonella food poisoning, cholera, and whooping cough. Bacteria in people's mouths can cause tooth decay. Many other kinds of bacteria live in your intestines or on your skin. These are harmless most of the time. But if your body isn't working properly, these bacteria may invade other parts and make you ill.

Viruses

Viruses are very small, much smaller than bacteria. They can't live on their own. They can survive only inside living cells of other bodies. Diseases caused by viruses include the common cold, influenza, measles, mumps, smallpox, yellow fever, and AIDS (Acquired Immune Deficiency Syndrome).

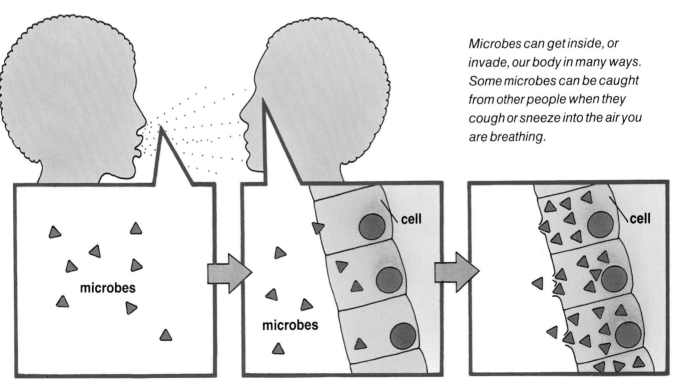

Microbes can get inside, or invade, our body in many ways. Some microbes can be caught from other people when they cough or sneeze into the air you are breathing.

1. When people cough and sneeze, microbes are pushed out into the air.

2. When you breathe in the microbes, the germs have a new body to invade.

3. The microbes attack the cells in your body, making you ill.

Defending your body

Your body has a way of fighting germs to protect you from diseases. Inside your body, there are millions of cells that kill invading microbes, such as bacteria and viruses. These cells make up your **immune system,** which keeps you healthy most of the time.

Your body makes the cells of your immune system in bone marrow. Large concentrations of these cells are found in certain internal organs, like the lymph nodes, the spleen, and the liver.

Different kinds of cells make up your immune system. Some move around your body in your blood. These are white blood cells known as **lymphocytes.** When they find invading microbes, they pass through the walls of the blood vessels to attack them.

Eating cells

Some immune cells kill germs by simply eating them. These cells are called **phagocytes,** which means "eating cells." They are also known as **macrophages.** Chemicals called **antibodies** stick to the microbes so that the phagocytes know where they are. If the virus that causes measles gets into your body, you will start making antibodies that stick all over the surface of the virus, like a label. The phagocytes can then spot the measles viruses and destroy them.

How do eating cells work?

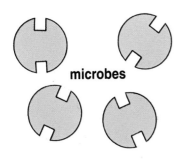

microbes

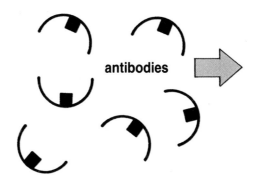

antibodies

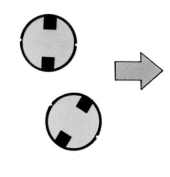

1. The microbes, such as bacteria or viruses, enter your body.

2. Your body makes special chemicals, called antibodies. These are released into the bloodstream.

3. An antibody recognizes a microbe and sticks to it.

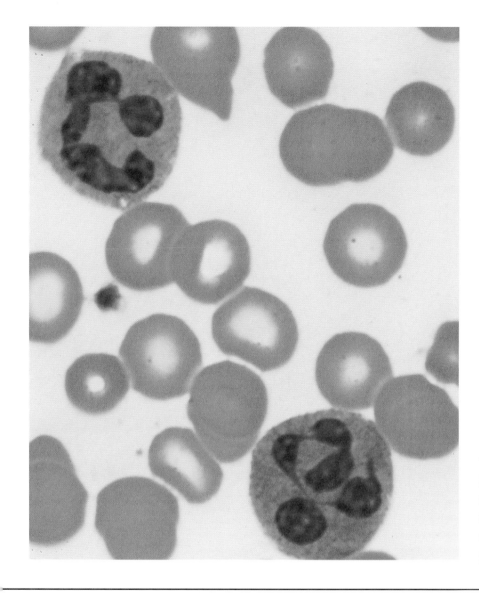

Your blood contains red cells and larger white cells. White blood cells are an important part of your body's immune system. They attack and destroy microbes that invade your body.

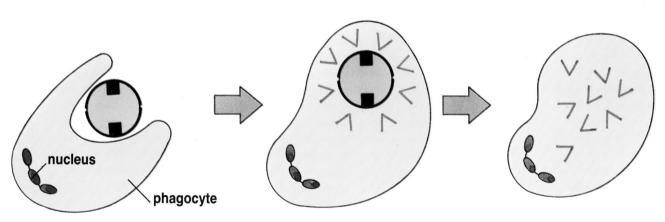

4. An eating cell, or phagocyte, starts to surround a microbe.

5. The phagocyte completely surrounds the microbe and digests it.

6. The microbe is destroyed, so the risk of disease becomes less.

Keeping disease away

Some diseases which are caused by viruses, such as cholera, will make you ill only once. How does your body stop you from having some diseases more than once?

The first time you have the virus, your body will take some time to make antibodies against it. That is why you are ill for a while. As soon as the antibodies start working, you begin to feel better. Once you are better, your body is repeatedly able to make the antibodies for that particular virus.

If the virus enters your body again, your body can make antibodies much more quickly than the first time. The antibodies defeat the virus without your knowing about it. You are now **immune** to that virus, which means that your body can protect itself against this disease in the future.

Changing viruses

Some viruses can't be kept out so easily. They keep changing their form. The antibody produced against the original form won't recognize the new form. Thus your body needs extra time to develop a new antibody for each form. The viruses that cause the common cold and influenza keep changing like this, so we have these illnesses again and again. The virus that causes AIDS can also change its form.

Special protection from disease

Doctors have a way of helping our bodies to fight against some diseases. This is done by giving people **vaccinations.** When you have a vaccination against cholera, a tiny amount of the cholera virus, which has been specially treated, is injected into your body through a needle. Your body then makes antibodies to fight the virus. So when the cholera virus tries to attack your body, you are immune to the disease that it causes.

Vaccinations are a major part of the worldwide fight against diseases, such as cholera, tuberculosis, and polio. Smallpox, the first disease for which a vaccine was used, has almost completely disappeared. But for some diseases, such as AIDS and the common cold, doctors still haven't found a vaccine.

In the United States, vaccinations are an important part of preventative medicine for children.

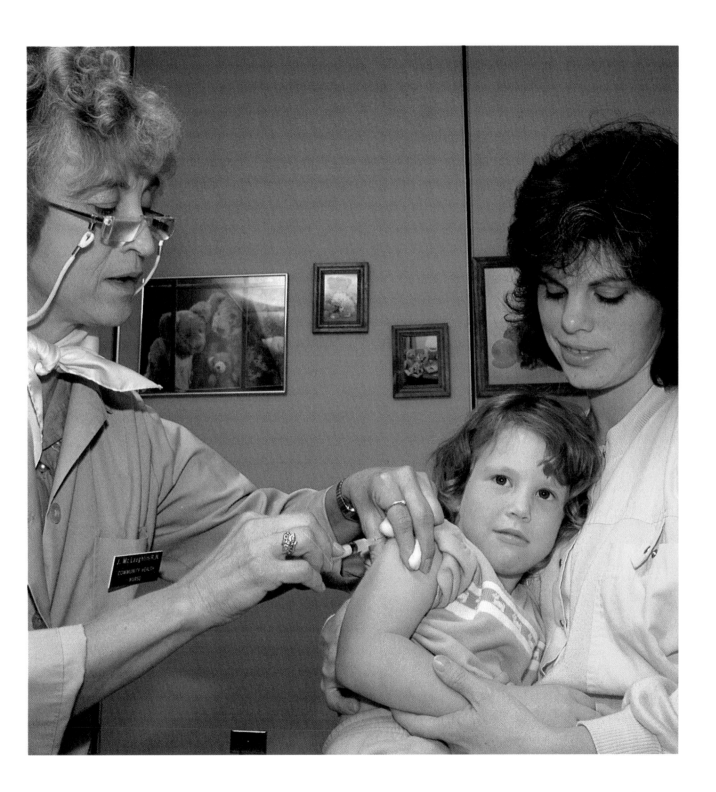

Find out more by looking at pages **48–49**

The larger invaders

You have seen how some diseases are caused by tiny microbes. Other diseases are caused by larger creatures called **protists** and also by worms. These larger invaders are sometimes more difficult to kill than the smaller ones.

Diseases caused by protists

Malaria and sleeping sickness are two diseases caused by protists. Protists are soft, jellylike creatures that usually need to be surrounded by plenty of water in order to survive. As our bodies contain lots of water, they can live inside us. Not all protists live inside people or other animals. Some live harmlessly in soil and water.

Protists are not as easily spread from one person to another as some microbes, such as bacteria and viruses. But they have special ways of infecting people. Some harmful protists are spread by biting insects. Tsetse flies spread sleeping sickness, and mosquitoes spread malaria and yellow fever.

When a mosquito bites a person, it sucks up blood. At the same time, it may infect the person's blood with the protist that causes yellow fever.

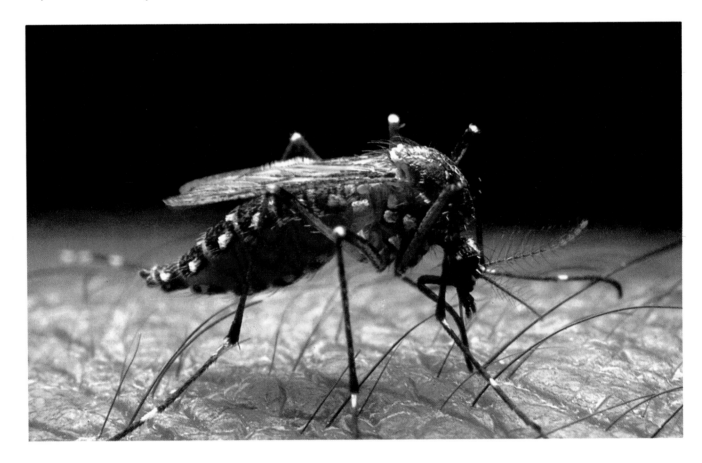

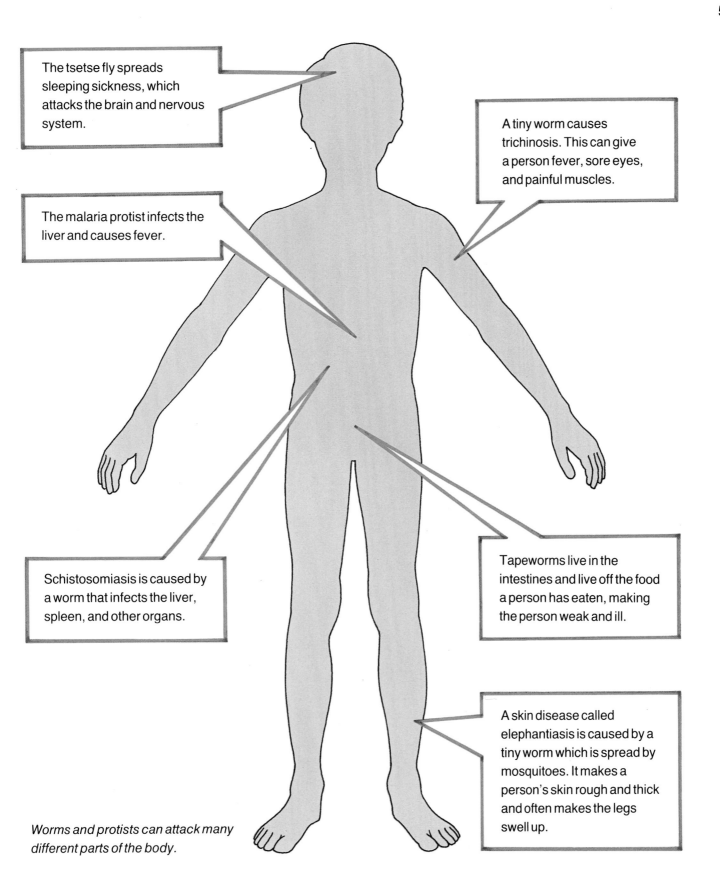

The tsetse fly spreads sleeping sickness, which attacks the brain and nervous system.

A tiny worm causes trichinosis. This can give a person fever, sore eyes, and painful muscles.

The malaria protist infects the liver and causes fever.

Schistosomiasis is caused by a worm that infects the liver, spleen, and other organs.

Tapeworms live in the intestines and live off the food a person has eaten, making the person weak and ill.

A skin disease called elephantiasis is caused by a tiny worm which is spread by mosquitoes. It makes a person's skin rough and thick and often makes the legs swell up.

Worms and protists can attack many different parts of the body.

Stop disease from spreading!

There are government and private agencies that are concerned with the public health. They help prevent disease by purifying local water supplies, overseeing garbage disposal, keeping sewers in working order, and trying to control environmental pollution. Doctors and hospitals provide many services that help in disease prevention, too.

But there are many ways in which you can also help to prevent disease. Here are some important things to remember that will help protect you and your family from disease.

Washing your hands

Many microbes are spread by feces. However careful you are, you get some microbes on your hands when you go to the toilet. Always wash your hands with soap and water afterwards.

Flies

Houseflies spread diseases when they land on food. Keep food covered up if there are flies about.

Pets

Pets can spread some diseases. Do not let a pet eat from your plate or lick your face around the mouth. Be careful about animal feces, too. If your pet uses part of the garden as a toilet, do not handle the soil there without gloves.

Water

Don't drink water from streams and rivers. Never drink pond or lake water. Before you swim anywhere, make sure that the water is free from harmful substances. If there is doubt don't go swimming.

Coughs and sneezes

If you sneeze when you have a cold, you are showering everyone around you with thousands of microbes. Cover your mouth when you cough, and sneeze into a handkerchief.

Keeping it to yourself

If you have a disease that can spread, try not to pass it on to anyone else! Stay away from other people as much as you can, until you are better.

Cuts and scratches

Be careful with cuts and scratches because they are open to microbes. Cover them up with a bandaid, especially if you are touching soil or swimming in a river. Cover up cuts if you are preparing food, because microbes can spread to the food.

Food

Always wash your hands before touching food. Always cook meat thoroughly. Do not keep cooked food for too long before eating it. Never store raw meat so that it can touch, or drip onto, cooked meat. It's a good idea to wash fruit and vegetables with clean water before you store them in the refrigerator or eat them. If you have a vegetable garden, don't let pets use it as a toilet.

The machine breaks down

Not all diseases are caused by things which invade our bodies. Some diseases occur because parts of our bodies simply stop working properly. Other diseases are caused by poisons in our food and drink, by lack of food, or even by the air we breathe. A disease may have many different causes. Sometimes the cause is unknown.

Diseases from birth

Some people are born with an illness that stays with them for their whole life. Other members of their family often suffer from the same problem. Many of these diseases can't be cured, but they can often be overcome in other ways. Some people have to stay on a special diet because they can't eat the foods that most people eat. Others have to take special medicines to keep their disease under control.

Allergies

Some people become ill when they come into contact with certain substances that are usually harmless. These substances can be dust, or pollen from plants. They make some people's bodies react to them as though they were harmful microbes. This causes a kind of illness called an **allergy**. Common allergies include hay fever, asthma, and some types of eczema.

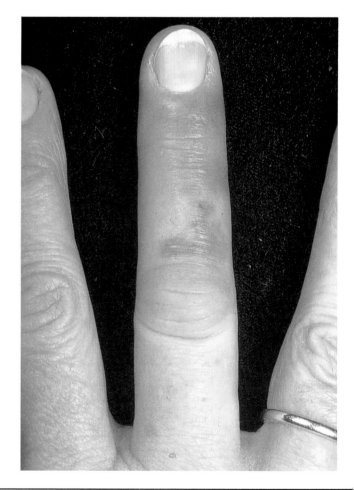

This finger has been stung by a bee. Allergy to the sting has made the finger red and swollen.

Cancer

Cancer is caused by cells that grow and divide without control. As uncontrolled divisions occur, a mass of cells is formed, called a **malignant tumor.** Doctors have discovered that certain chemicals in the world around us can make the growth of these tumors more likely. These chemicals are called **carcinogens.** Some people think that many of the chemicals that are added to food are carcinogens. This is why many people are careful to eat more natural food.

Cure from the rain forests

The tropical rain forests provide scientists with an enormous variety of plants. Some of these plants contain special chemicals that can be used as medicines. Scientists in the United States have found some tropical rain forest plants that might be used to fight against cancer.

About 30 years ago, scientists who were trying to find a cure for cancer investigated a plant called the **rosy periwinkle.** This grows in the tropical forests of Madagascar, an island off the coast of Africa.

For many years, local healers had used this plant as a medicine. The scientists found that chemicals in the rosy periwinkle helped to treat cancer. It was especially useful for treating children with cancer of the blood, known as leukemia. Treatment using the rosy periwinkle has meant that more people can now be cured of cancer.

Chemicals in the rosy periwinkle can help to treat leukemia.

People can buy many kinds of food at this market in Kathmandu, in Nepal. You should eat a wide variety of food to keep your body healthy. Different foods provide different things your body needs.

Taking care of your body

You've seen that your body is like a wonderful machine, and you've found out how it works. Each part of your body has a special job to do. But in order for each part to work properly and in harmony with all the other parts, you must take care of your body.

To stay healthy, you need to eat meals that contain a balanced choice of foods. You need to take some kind of exercise regularly. And you must also rest, to allow your body to regain energy. It is important that you wash and keep yourself clean, to reduce the chances of catching a disease or an infection.

Eating the right foods

Many people are lucky enough to be able to eat all the right foods they need to keep alive and healthy. While you are growing, you need plenty of protein. This is found in foods such as fish, meat, milk, eggs, beans, and nuts. You also need to eat fresh fruit and vegetables. You should eat regular meals and not go for long periods of time without eating.

Taking regular exercise

As well as eating the right foods, you must keep your muscles and joints healthy by doing lots of exercise. Regular exercise keeps your body strong and fit. It keeps the blood vessels healthy and makes the blood reach every part of your body. It helps you avoid putting on extra weight. The best exercise comes from cycling, running, walking, or swimming.

Keeping clean

Make sure you keep yourself and your surroundings clean. This will help prevent bacteria, viruses, protists, and larger invaders from spreading through the environment and infecting you and others. Daily washing keeps your body free from dirt and prevents skin infections. The areas of your house where you eat and wash should always be kept clean.

Preventing illness

You can also be protected against some illnesses by being vaccinated. You can have vaccinations which will make you immune to certain viruses, such as measles, tuberculosis, and polio. There are laws that require vaccinations. If schools don't offer a program of vaccination, then parents see to their own children.

Make sure you clean your teeth every day. Don't eat too many sugary foods, because they harm your teeth. It's a good idea to visit a dentist and have your teeth checked regularly.

Sleeping

Everyone needs sleep. Although the norm is eight hours a day, some people may need more, and others may require less. Sleep helps your body to recuperate, particularly the brain and the nervous system. Without sleep, you have less energy and feel tired. After hard work or exercise, you need to rest and relax. Relaxation can be just as important as sleep in helping you keep healthy.

A playground like this is an exciting place to run around and climb. You don't need a special place to play in, but make sure that where you play is safe.

COMMUNICATION

Exchanging messages

Every minute of every day, all over the world, people are sending messages to each other. Just think of the number of different ways of receiving messages in your own home. There are radio and television. You may have a cassette player or record player with which you can play back recorded messages. The telephone lets you send messages as well as receive them.

Getting the message

Sending and receiving messages is called **communicating.** People communicate with each other in many different ways. They can speak to each other, make gestures with their hands or faces, or even write a note. It is easy to communicate with someone who is in the same room with you, but more difficult if that person is a mile away. In the past, people have sent messages over long distances by using drums or flashing lights or even smoke signals.

Talking with electricity

One hundred and fifty years ago, people would have been amazed if they had known that we would talk to people thousands of miles away, receive pictures in our own homes from space, and even send instant copies of letters or photographs from one place to another.

Today, modern systems are very rapid and reliable. We use electricity to send and receive messages by telephone, facsimile, telex, radio, and television. This method of exchanging messages is called **telecommunications.** It all began with the invention of the electric telegraph. The electric telegraph marked the beginning of the telecommunications age that we live in today.

Telecommunications has made it possible for people to communicate in split seconds over long distances.

Lung power

We talk, sing, or shout so that other people can hear us. But how does the sound we make reach them? The sound of our voices travels through the air as **waves.** These are tiny movements of air, called **vibrations.** You can feel these vibrations if you shout close to a piece of paper placed on your hand. The sound waves will hit the paper and make it vibrate. As vibrations spread out and move away from us, they gradually become weaker and fainter.

Catch those sound waves

Find out how to throw your voice and catch sound.

You will need:

2 triangles of stiff cardboard

a stone or pebble

scissors

adhesive tape

1. Make a megaphone by folding one corner of the cardboard across to the other. Curve the cardboard around so that two sides meet and make a cone.

2. Tape the edges together. Snip off the point to make a hole. Now make another cone exactly the same to use as an ear trumpet.

3. Go to a park or open space with a friend. Stand facing each other but quite far apart. Then shout out something to your friend. If your friend can hear you, he or she should step back. Keep doing this until your friend can no longer hear you. Mark this distance with a stone.

Traveling sound

If you shout louder, the sound waves you make will be louder and will travel farther. But even the loudest sound soon dies away. A simple instrument like a megaphone can make sound travel farther because it directs the sound waves and keeps them from spreading out so much. An ear trumpet enables you to hear sounds better. Its funnel shape collects the sound waves together, so that they become stronger. Why do cheerleaders use megaphones?

4. Now try it again. This time, ask your friend to cup both hands behind the ears. How far from the stone is your friend?

sound waves

5. Now try shouting through your megaphone. Does this carry your voice even farther?

6. Ask your friend to use the ear trumpet. What difference does this make?

sound waves

Find out more by looking at
pages **72–73**
      92–93

Pass the message

If you receive a message and pass it on to someone else, you are acting as a **relay.** Relays are useful for sending messages over long distances.

In telecommunications, relays pick up a signal and make it stronger before passing it on. Without relays, the signal would be too weak to understand by the time it reached the end of its journey.

Pony Express

One of the most famous relay systems was the Pony Express, which carried mail from St Joseph, Missouri, in the United States of America, over the mountains to Sacramento, California. This was in 1860 and 1861, before there were railways or telegraph lines across North America. Pony Express riders used fast horses or ponies. The horses were changed every 10–15 miles (16–24 kilometers). Each rider traveled 74 miles (120 kilometers) or more in a working day. So a message got through much more quickly than it would have with a single messenger. But by October 1861, the transcontinental telegraph was completed, and the Pony Express was no longer needed.

Riders of the Pony Express traveled in relays day and night in all kinds of weather. A package could travel the entire 1,962-mile (3,164-kilometer) trail in 10 days or less.

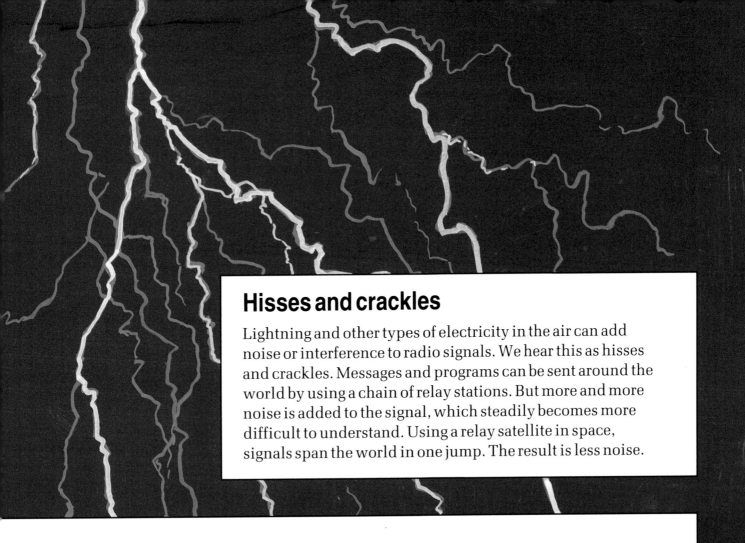

Hisses and crackles

Lightning and other types of electricity in the air can add noise or interference to radio signals. We hear this as hisses and crackles. Messages and programs can be sent around the world by using a chain of relay stations. But more and more noise is added to the signal, which steadily becomes more difficult to understand. Using a relay satellite in space, signals span the world in one jump. The result is less noise.

The relay game

Playing the relay game shows how easy it is for relayed messages to be changed or misunderstood.

Make up a group of eight or more people in a circle. One person whispers a 10-word message to the next, who whispers it on, and so on around the circle. No one may whisper the message more than once.

When the message has gone around the circle, the last person calls it out. The person who started calls out their message.

You can make the game more difficult by starting two messages going in opposite directions at the same time.

Signalling

Throughout history, armies and navies have sent messages across battlefields. Simple orders like "Advance" or "Retreat" could be given by bugle calls or cannon-fire. But sending reports of the battle back to headquarters needed a different system.

Semaphore

During the 1790's, a Frenchman called Claude Chappe invented a signalling system called **semaphore.** This was a system of sending signals by means of two jointed arms at the tops of tall posts. These arms could be moved to different positions to show different letters of the alphabet. Each semaphore station was built on a hill so that it could be seen, using a telescope, from the next station in any direction. In this way, messages could be relayed over long distances from one station to the next. Semaphore stations on the coast would send messages to ships at sea.

Signal for battle

On the battlefield, there might not be a semaphore station, but messages could be sent by stationing signallers with large flags on nearby hills. They used the same code as the semaphore arms. An expert signaller could send or receive up to 25 letters a minute, and messages could be relayed nearly 155 miles (250 kilometers) in 15 minutes.

A semaphore signaller holds two flags in different positions for each letter of the alphabet. He can also communicate other signals such as errors and numbers.

A B C D E F G H I J K

R S T U V W X Y

Signals at sea

Sailors signalled to each other with flags. The picture shows one of the most famous naval signals in British history. It was sent by Admiral Lord Nelson to the British fleet before the Battle of Trafalgar, in 1805. It read "England expects every man will do his duty."

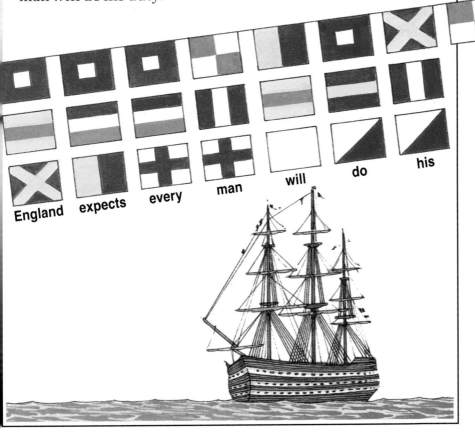

England expects every man will do his

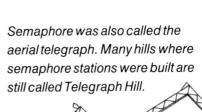

D U T Y

Semaphore was also called the aerial telegraph. Many hills where semaphore stations were built are still called Telegraph Hill.

L M N O P Q

Z Error End of word Numbers follow Attention Answering sign

Dots and dashes

In 1832, an American artist sailed home from Europe. He had spent some time painting in Europe and hoped to sell his pictures when he arrived home. His name was Samuel Morse.

Talking through wires

The journey on the ship was to change Samuel Morse's life. He met a young chemist from Boston, named Charles Jackson, who showed him how an electromagnet works. Morse became interested in electricity and in the idea of sending messages along electric wires. Morse was one of the first people to make an **electric telegraph.** An electric telegraph uses an electric current to send messages along a wire.

Operators of this electric telegraph machine sent messages down the line in Morse Code.

A • ▬
B ▬ • • •
C ▬ • ▬ •
D ▬ • •
E •
F • • ▬ •
G ▬ ▬ •
H • • • •
I • •
J • ▬ ▬ ▬
K ▬ • ▬
L • ▬ • •
M ▬ ▬
N ▬ •
O ▬ ▬ ▬
P • ▬ ▬ •
Q ▬ ▬ • ▬
R • ▬ •
S • • •
T ▬
U • • ▬
V • • • ▬
W • ▬ ▬
X ▬ • • ▬
Y ▬ • ▬ ▬
Z ▬ ▬ • •

Morse Code

This telegraph was not what made Morse famous. He gave his name to the code of dots and dashes which he invented. Until this time, most long distance messages were sent by semaphore. The problem with the electric telegraph was that an electric current can be arranged in only two ways. Either the current is flowing and it is "On," or it is "Off." Somehow a way had to be found of using the flow of current to make a code that could be sent along the wires.

Morse's answer was to make codes for different letters and numbers out of short and long bursts, or **pulses,** of electric current. He called these **dots** and **dashes.** Using dots and dashes in different orders made the different codes. The Morse "key" which makes the pulses is a kind of switch that turns the current on and off. Messages sent by electric telegraph would be marked by the receiving machine on a moving strip of paper. Then the telegraph operator would decode the dots and dashes into ordinary letters and numbers. But operators who used Morse Code soon became skilled at "reading" the messages directly from the clicks made by the machine. The **international,** or **continental, Morse Code** is shown opposite.

The emergency signal in Morse Code, SOS, is known to sailors all over the world. They use it to call for urgent help if a ship is in danger.

• • • ▬ ▬ ▬ • • •

1 • ▬ ▬ ▬ ▬
2 • • ▬ ▬ ▬
3 • • • ▬ ▬
4 • • • • ▬
5 • • • • •
6 ▬ • • • •
7 ▬ ▬ • • •
8 ▬ ▬ ▬ • •
9 ▬ ▬ ▬ ▬ •
0 ▬ ▬ ▬ ▬ ▬

Morse invented a different dot and dash pattern for each letter and number.

Communicating by light

Sometimes when you are in open country, you may catch a flash of sunlight on the windshield of a car many miles away. The windshield acts like a mirror and reflects the light. You have probably shone a flashlight beam against a wall or ceiling and watched the spot of light. Cover the mirror or flashlight with your hand, and the light disappears.

Heliograph

Put these two ideas together, and you have one of the oldest ways of communicating in the world—signalling by the light of the sun. The ancient Greeks signaled to each other in this way. They used an instrument called a **heliograph.** The name comes from the ancient Greek words for "sun" and "writing." A heliograph can be seen up to 30 miles (48 kilometers) away on a clear day without a telescope.

The modern heliograph is mounted on a tripod, like a camera. It can turn in any direction. The mirror flashes when it is directed at the sun and can then be dipped away or covered with a shutter. If the signaler wants to send a message in a direction away from the sun, a second mirror is used to reflect light on to the first. Heliograph messages are sent in Morse Code.

You can send heliograph messages using a simple mirror. Tilt the mirror so that it catches the sun's rays. Then reflect the rays towards your friend.

Messages in the dark

A heliograph can be used only in the daytime when the sun is shining. But at night, light messages can be sent using an Aldis lamp. This is a powerful searchlight. It has a shutter that can be moved to block out the light and also make the dots and dashes of Morse code.

The Aldis lamp has a shutter which breaks up the light into Morse dots and dashes.

At night, lighthouses flash codes of light to warn ships away from a dangerous coastline.

Messages over the wire

By the 1850's, the electric telegraph had brought a great leap forward in communications. For the first time, people could exchange messages almost instantly over long distances. The telegraph could be used by day or night in any kind of weather. The operator could send a message to a number of different places at the same time.

You will need:

8 pieces of wood about 4 in. × 2 in. × 1 in. (10 cm × 5 cm × 2.5 cm) thick

steel screws, screwdriver

nails, hammer

two steel hinges 2 in. × 1 in. (5 cm × 2.5 cm)

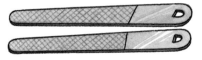

two thin metal nail files

a small piece of cloth

some thin, plastic-coated wire

one 6-volt battery

Make a two-way telegraph

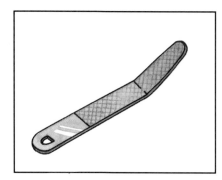

1. Use a file to make a telegraph key.

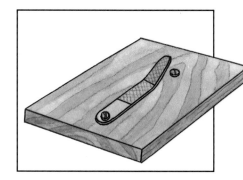

2. Screw the key to one end of the wood, but do not tighten the screw yet. Put another screw all the way into the board under the other end of the key.

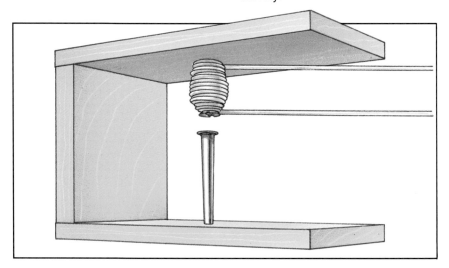

3. Make a coil by winding plastic-coated wire 50 times around a screw. Screw the coil into the center of a piece of wood.

4. Make the sounder by nailing the piece of wood containing the coil to two other pieces of wood, as in the picture.

The key and the sounder

The two parts of the telegraph are the **key,** which is used to send a message, and the **sounder** which receives it. They are joined by wire. For two-way communication, each operator must have a key and also a sounder that is attached to a different key.

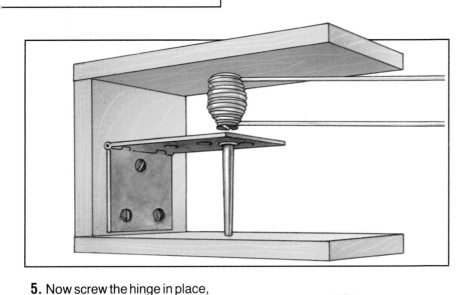

Test the system by pressing key 1 so that the free end of the metal file touches the screw underneath it. This should make sounder 1 click. Test again with key 2 and sounder 2. If everything works, you are ready to start sending messages in Morse Code to another operator.

When you press a key, the current flowing through the wire coil makes the screw magnetic. It attracts the free arm of the hinge, which moves upwards and makes a click. When the key is released, the hinge falls back.

5. Now screw the hinge in place, supported by the nail. Leave a gap of less than .25 inches (.6 millimeters) between the hinge and the coil screw.

6. Make two keys and two sounders. Connect them to the battery as in the picture. Now tighten the screws at the fixed end of the metal keys.

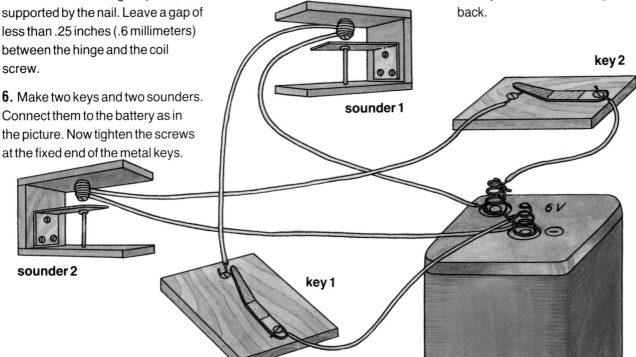

sounder 1

key 2

sounder 2

key 1

6 V

Sending printed messages

As towns and cities began to be linked by telegraph lines, engineers realized that these could be used in other ways.

When Samuel Morse invented the Morse Code, his idea was to invent a machine that could write a message in the dots and dashes using an ordinary pen. The dots and dashes would then be decoded by the telegraph operator and written out in "plain language." By 1844, telegraph messages were recorded in Morse Code on paper tape.

By 1874, the first **typewriters** were being made in the United States of America. It was not long before engineers began to wonder if typewriters could be used to make telegraphy easier. Telegraph wires could carry a different electric signal for each letter of the alphabet and each number. So typewriters linked by telegraph could send and receive messages in plain language, not in Morse Code.

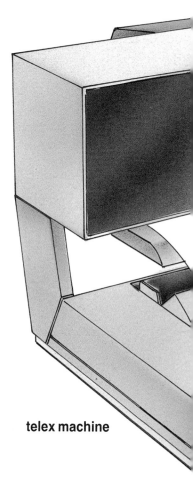

telex machine

This photograph has been sent by 'wire' to a newspaper office. You can see the lines which show that it has been scanned by the machine. The result is not as good as if a photographic print had been used, but wire is often the only way of sending pictures of urgent news.

The teleprinter

The new machine brought together two great inventions of the 1800's—the telegraph and the typewriter. It was at first called a printing telegraph, but this was shortened to "teleprinter" and later to **"telex."** The operator sat at an electromechanical typewriter and typed in the message. Each key sent a different set of electric signals over the wires to the receiving machine, which printed out the message.

Another type of teleprinter turned each letter into a code made up of holes punched out of a paper tape. The code was then sent over the wires as a series of electric signals. The code was copied by the receiving machine, which turned it back into a typed message. Paper tape signals could be passed down the wires at high speed.

Telegraphy can also be used to send pictures. A machine scans the picture and converts the image into a set of electric signals. A similar machine at the other end decodes the signals and prints the picture out on special paper. The modern version of this is the **facsimile,** or **fax,** machine. It uses telephone lines and works much faster than earlier versions.

fax machine

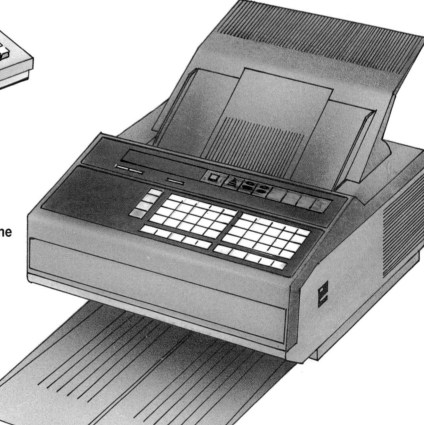

Newspapers use telex machines to receive news from all over the world. Most modern offices now use fax machines to send and receive messages and pictures.

How the telephone works

Over 100 years ago, an American scientist called Alexander Graham Bell was sure that electricity could be used to carry voices over long distances. But how could the sound of voices be turned into electricity? Eventually, after many years of hard work, Bell found the answer. His invention was the first kind of **telephone.** It completely changed people's lives. Have you spoken to someone very far away on the telephone? It's amazing how clear their voice is — even from the other side of the world.

Voices, like other sounds, make vibrations in the air called **sound waves.** Sound waves are different from each other. Some are loud, some are soft, and some vibrate much more quickly than others. This means that each sound wave can be turned into an electric signal, which can travel along a wire.

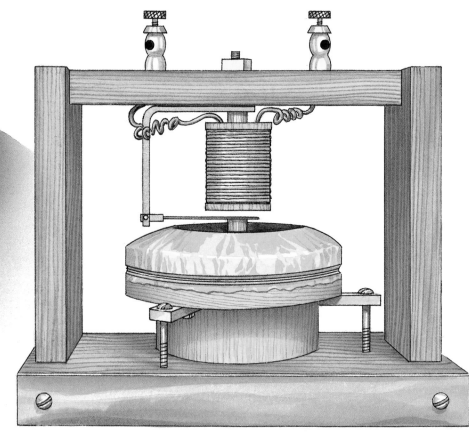

This is the first telephone, invented by Alexander Graham Bell in 1876. The first one-way long-distance call was made in Ontario, Canada, between two towns 8 miles (13 kilometers) apart.

What's inside the telephone?

When you speak into the telephone, the sound waves of your voice make a disk called the **diaphragm** vibrate at various speeds. As the diaphragm moves in one direction, it pushes carbon granules placed behind it closer together. This allows an electric current to pass through the carbon granules easily. As the diaphragm moves in the opposite direction, the electric current becomes weaker. These changes in the electric current happen very quickly, as your voice vibrates the diaphragm. The current flows along a telephone wire to the earpiece of another telephone.

There, an electromagnet pulls a diaphragm in the earpiece of the receiving telephone. As the electric current becomes stronger or weaker, the diaphragm moves in or out. This movement makes the air vibrate to produce the sound waves duplicating your voice, which the listener hears.

The earpiece of the telephone contains a thin, round metal disk called a diaphragm. Behind this diaphragm is an electromagnet, which behaves like a magnet when an electric current flows through it.

diaphragm

electromagnet

permanent magnet

The mouthpiece of the telephone contains a microphone. This has a thin metal disk or diaphragm. Behind the disk are carbon granules, which allow an electric current to flow.

diaphragm

Connecting your call

There are millions of telephones in the world. Each one can be connected with any of the others. Each telephone in a town or district is joined by wires to the local telephone exchange. The telephone exchanges in different towns or districts are linked together by more wires or by trunk cables. Over longer distances, radio transmitters and receivers, or even space satellites, are used.

Dialing a number

Every telephone has its own special number. By dialing this number you get through to the telephone at the other end of the line. Dialing the number sends electric pulses along the telephone wire. The number of pulses is the same as the number you dial. So if you dial "7," seven pulses will travel along the line. Modern telephones are rotary or push-button operated. **Rotary telephones** have an electric switch inside them which creates the electric signals sent over the line. **Push-button telephones** use musical notes to create the electric signals. Each note stands for a different number on the telephone.

Modern exchanges have electronic circuits to connect phone calls. The electric signals or musical tones travel through the exchange electronically. As electronic switches have no moving parts, they are reliable, quiet, and small. This is very important in a large exchange where thousands of calls need to be connected at any moment.

After you've dialed or pressed the buttons, the signals travel over the line to the local telephone exchange. Inside the telephone exchange, switchgear connects the many thousands of calls coming through each day.

83

Find out more by looking at
pages **80–81**
      84–85
      88–89

Putting you through

When the electric signals reach the telephone exchange, automatic switches send more electric signals over the lines to the number you dialed. When the telephone rings at the other end, the person who answers it picks up the handset, or receiver, as it is usually called. This automatically stops the telephone from ringing and the conversation can begin. Your words are then transmitted over the line by another set of electric signals.

By land, sea, or air

International and other long-distance calls may pass through many exchanges before the final connection is made. The signals can travel from one exchange to the next by land line, underwater cable, or by radio satellite. Radio relay systems use superhigh frequency radio waves called **microwaves.** Microwaves can be beamed directly between the exchanges. Or they may go through a communications satellite in orbit thousands of miles above the earth.

telephone exchange

telephone exchange

telephone exchange

Find out more by looking at pages **82–83**

Sharing the line

Just suppose that one million people in one city wanted to speak to one million people in another city—all at the same time. Then one million wires or radio links would be needed to join them together. There simply isn't room for all these wires or radio stations. Instead, the links between the telephone exchanges are shared, which means that fewer wires or radio links are needed.

Long-distance call

When you talk over a long distance, you are sharing your link with many other people. You cannot hear their conversations because each conversation is carried on a different frequency (rate of vibration). This means that many conversations use one wire or a single radio link, but they do not interfere with each other.

The line between these two telephone exchanges is shared between the red, yellow, and blue callers. Follow each color from the caller, through the two exchanges, and to the correct receiver.

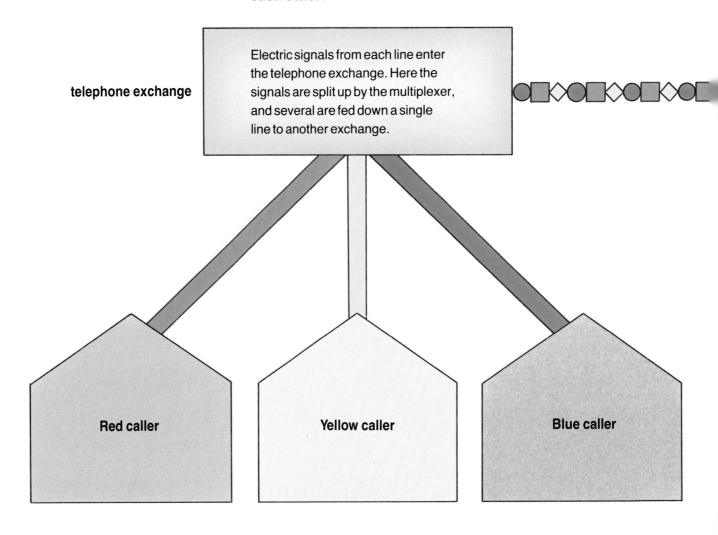

telephone exchange

Electric signals from each line enter the telephone exchange. Here the signals are split up by the multiplexer, and several are fed down a single line to another exchange.

Red caller

Yellow caller

Blue caller

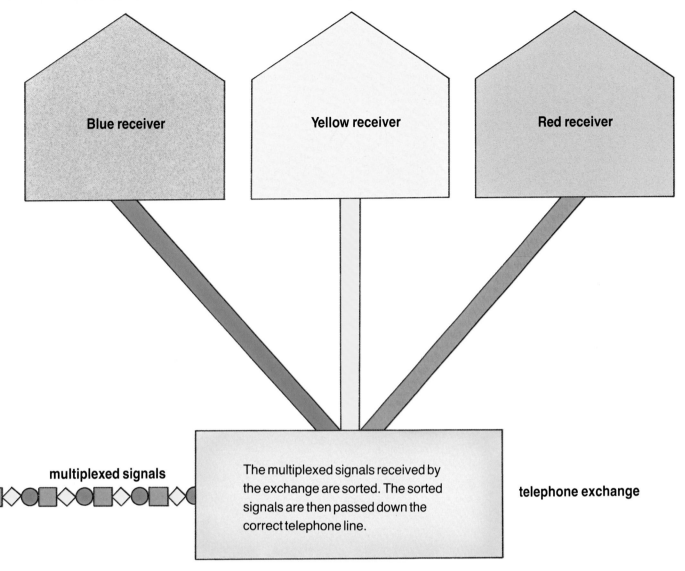

Blue receiver

Yellow receiver

Red receiver

multiplexed signals

The multiplexed signals received by the exchange are sorted. The sorted signals are then passed down the correct telephone line.

telephone exchange

Coding your call

When you speak into your telephone, the vibrations from your voice are turned into varied electric currents. These electric currents—the signals—travel over the wire. At the exchange, the vibrating electric signals are turned into a code. The coded electric signals are not vibrating, but they are a string of pulses. It is like turning a switch on and off very quickly. The coded signals from different conversations are divided up into pieces by a **multiplexer.** These pieces are then sent one after the other through the wire or radio link between exchanges.

At the receiving exchange, the pieces are sorted out and put back together again by another multiplexer. Each complete coded signal is then decoded and sent over the line to the person you are calling. What you hear is the voice of your friend as clearly as if that person were nearby.

The string telephone

A string telephone does not need electricity to make it work. It works by changing the sound of your voice into vibrations, which travel along the string. When they reach the other end, the vibrations are changed back into sound again.

You will need:

two empty plastic cups

a ball of thin, strong string

Over and out

When you are using the string telephone, you will have to work out a way of telling the person at the other end when to listen and when to speak. One way is to copy the system that radio operators use. When you have finished speaking and are ready for an answer, you say 'Over.' This is the signal for the person at the other end to speak. When you come to the end of the conversation, you say 'Out'.

If there are three of you, you can make a third string telephone and use it as an extension. Tie the string to the first line in a convenient place.

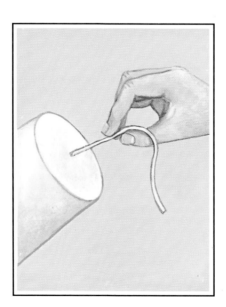

1. Make a small hole in the end of each plastic cup and thread an end of the string through the hole.

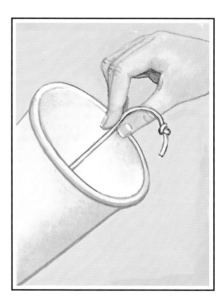

2. Tie a knot on the inside to keep it in place. The plastic cup acts as both mouthpiece and earpiece.

Find out more by looking at pages **80–81**

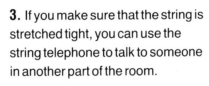

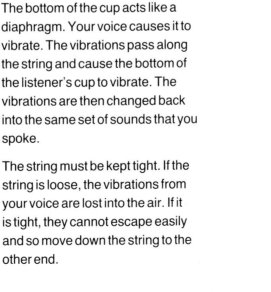

3. If you make sure that the string is stretched tight, you can use the string telephone to talk to someone in another part of the room.

The bottom of the cup acts like a diaphragm. Your voice causes it to vibrate. The vibrations pass along the string and cause the bottom of the listener's cup to vibrate. The vibrations are then changed back into the same set of sounds that you spoke.

The string must be kept tight. If the string is loose, the vibrations from your voice are lost into the air. If it is tight, they cannot escape easily and so move down the string to the other end.

Find out more by looking at pages **82–83**

Wires under the sea

You may have watched workmen digging up the streets of your town to repair electric cables. You have probably seen telephone and telegraph wires strung between pylons or poles from city to city. But how can people communicate from one continent to another? Long cables have to be sunk deep under the sea.

Laying cables

It sounds easy to unroll a giant reel of insulated cable into the sea, letting it sink to the seabed. But the first engineers to lay underwater cables soon discovered all kinds of problems. Rocks on the seabed damage the insulation. The cable can easily break when it is being laid. Once in place, it can be damaged by ships' anchors, fishing nets, or sea creatures.

The British steamship S.S. Great Eastern laid the first successful transatlantic cable in 1866. The cable stretched from Ireland to Newfoundland in Canada.

Today transatlantic cable links are laid deep under the sea by submersible vehicles such as the Seadog.

Seadog

Engineers solved these problems by inventing a special underwater vehicle called the **Seadog.** The Seadog is a submersible tractor and digger. As it moves along the ocean bed, it digs a trench and lays down the cable. Once the cable becomes buried in the seabed, it is safe from fishing nets and rocks. There are no people on board the Seadog. It is linked to the cable ship and worked by remote control.

Messages on waves

Messages can be sent over long distances by telegraph and telephone. Until a hundred years ago, long-distance messages had to be relayed by wire. Then scientists discovered **radio waves.** Radio waves can travel through empty space.

In 1895, an Italian scientist, Guglielmo Marconi, was the first scientist to send radio signals through the the air. At first, radio messages were sent in Morse Code. Experimental radio broadcasts began about 1910.

Vibrating signals

Radio waves are electric signals that vibrate millions of times a second as they travel. Radio waves travel at a speed of 186,282 miles (299,792 kilometers) per second—that's the speed of light.

Imagine that you could see radio waves as they passed you. Some radio waves vibrate very frequently. They have a high **frequency.** Some radio waves vibrate more strongly. They have a high **amplitude.** Some waves have a low frequency. The distance between one low-frequency vibration and the next is longer than that between two high-frequency waves. The low-frequency wave will have a longer **wavelength.**

You cannot see or hear radio waves, but there are many different radio waves travelling between transmitters and receivers.

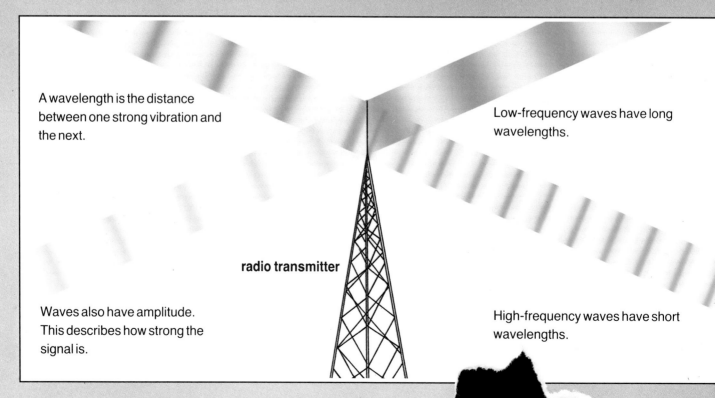

A wavelength is the distance between one strong vibration and the next.

Low-frequency waves have long wavelengths.

radio transmitter

Waves also have amplitude. This describes how strong the signal is.

High-frequency waves have short wavelengths.

A radio transmitter can send out the different types of radio waves through the air and into space, where satellites can beam the radio waves back to a receiving station on earth.

Radio broadcast

When radio waves are broadcast, they travel over different distances. Some waves, called **ground waves,** travel parallel to the earth's surface, trapped between the earth and a layer of the atmosphere called the ionosphere. Another type of wave, called **sky wave,** bounces back off the ionosphere during the daytime when the ionosphere is dense. Other waves, called UHF and VHF, can travel through the ionosphere and can be relayed by satellite.

satellite

Sky waves can travel over long distances. They do this by bouncing off the ionosphere. But sky-wave radio signals are difficult to receive at night, as the ionosphere is not dense enough without sunlight.

Ground waves travel parallel to the earth's surface. Ground waves are trapped between the surface of the earth and the ionosphere.

ionosphere

earth

UHF and VHF waves travel in straight lines as far as the horizon. But if they are directed towards the sky, they can travel through the ionosphere. Satellites in space can direct the waves back to earth.

Medium waves also follow the earth's surface but do not travel as far as ground waves.

92

Find out more by looking at
pages **82–83**
     106–107

More about radio waves

In its early days, radio was called "wireless." Unlike the telegraph and the telephone, it did not need wires to send messages. Radio signals can travel almost anywhere—even through space. But how does radio work? At the radio station, there is a **transmitter** connected to an **aerial.** The transmitter makes a radio signal which the aerial sends out. The main part of the radio signal is called the **carrier wave.** It is like an empty, invisible road between the station and your radio.

Transmitting signals

When the station broadcasts a program, it changes the music or speech sounds into electric signals and sends them out on the carrier wave. A radio **receiver** "separates" the signals from the carrier and turns them back into sounds.

Try throwing a pebble into the middle of a pond. The splash sends waves towards the edge. These are like a carrier wave. If you throw a second pebble into the pond, the second splash will change the pattern of waves from the first pebble. In the same way, the electric signals made from sounds being broadcast change the pattern of the carrier wave.

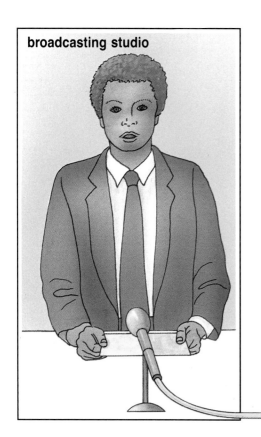

broadcasting studio

In the broadcasting studio, the speaker's voice is turned into electric signals. These are passed on to a transmitter. Here the signal is added to a carrier wave before being sent over the air.

transmitter

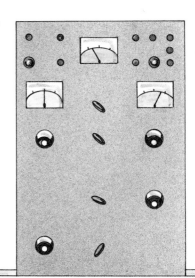

aerial

Altering the carrier wave

When the carrier wave is carrying these electric signals, it is known as a modulated carrier. The M in AM and FM stands for "modulation." Since many radios are able to pick up AM and FM broadcasting, you will see AM and FM written on the controls of these radios.

AM picks up broadcasts on the short-, medium-, or long-wave bands of a radio set. These broadcasts are known as Amplitude Modulation (AM) because they alter the strength of the carrier wave.

Frequency Modulation (FM) works on a Very High Frequency waveband (VHF) and changes the frequency of the wave.

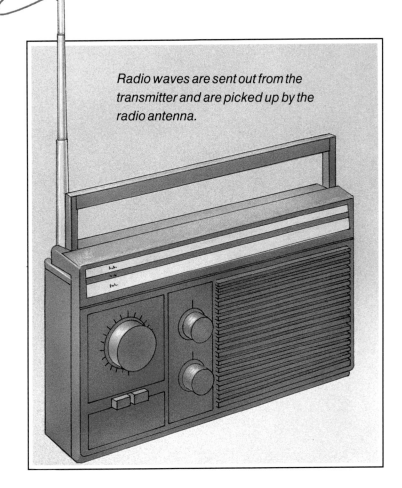

Radio waves are sent out from the transmitter and are picked up by the radio antenna.

Tuning in

This is a radio that can pick up long-wave, medium-wave, and short-wave signals and VHF. The numbers show the frequencies which can be received. A switch at the far right allows you to choose a particular waveband.

When a radio is tuned to the medium-wave, for example, it picks up only medium-wave signals. These pass into the radio through the antenna. All the signals, except the chosen one, pass through the radio unheard.

If you switch on the radio and turn the tuning knob, you can hear programs from many different stations. Some are local programs, broadcast only in the area where you live. Others are national, broadcast all over the country. Some may come from other countries. Others are broadcast all over the world. With so many radio programs, how does your radio find the one you have chosen?

First, the radio **antenna** picks up all the available signals. By turning the tuning knob on your radio, you can then select a waveband. Wavebands are divided into long, medium, and short wavebands or VHF (Very High Frequency).

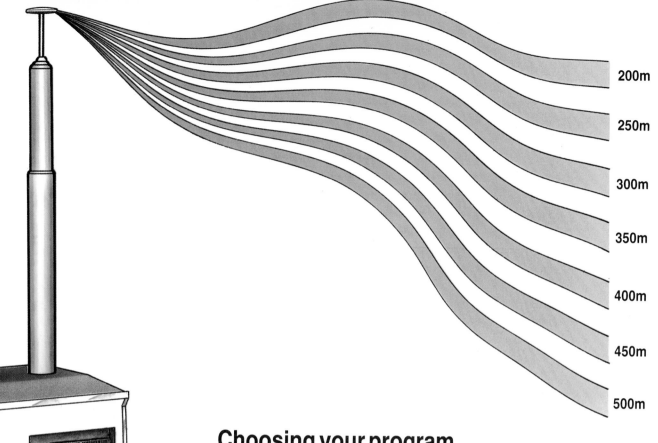

200m
250m
300m
350m
400m
450m
500m

FM
SW2   AM
       SW1
   BAND

FINE TUNING

Choosing your program

Supposing you want to listen to a program on the medium waveband. Press a switch or turn a knob to tune the radio to the medium waveband. Now the radio will pick up only those stations that are transmitting on this waveband.

Each radio station transmits on its own wavelength. If you want to hear a station transmitting on a wavelength of 1,000 feet (300 meters), you turn the tuning knob so that 1,000 (300) is marked on the dial. This changes the current flowing inside the radio so that it sorts out radio waves of the chosen length. All the other radio signals pass through your radio unheard.

Some radios have "pre-set" tuning. This means that you can set the radio to receive signals on a number of different wavelengths and then choose the program you want by pressing a button. This is particularly useful on car radios. The driver can find a program and still concentrate on driving.

Another type of radio can "hunt" through the wavelengths until it finds the station giving the strongest and clearest signal. This is useful for long-distance drivers who want to go on listening to a program which is broadcast on different wavelengths in different parts of the country.

Strengthening the signal

As radio waves travel away from the transmitter, they grow weaker. If the signals they carry are to be changed into sounds inside your radio, they have to be made stronger again once they reach the radio. There are two reasons why radio signals need to be strong and clear. First, they have to be quite strong to make the radio's speaker or headphones work. The second reason is that there is always electrical interference in the air. Unless the signals are clear and strong, this interference can cause an annoying background noise.

The amplifier

The part of the radio that makes the signals stronger is called the **amplifier.** Amplifiers strengthen the signal. They also "clean" it, by acting like a filter. They only allow the program sounds to come through. They cut out unwanted sounds that come from atmospheric interference.

Making waves

Try this experiment to see how waves are amplified.

1. Jiggle one end of a rope while a friend holds the other end still. You'll see a wave shape pass along the rope.

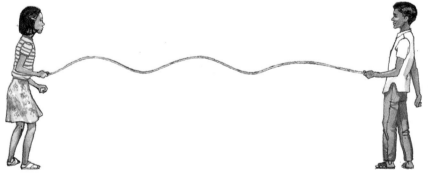

2. Now ask your friend to jiggle the rope at the same time, in step with you. The waves will get bigger.

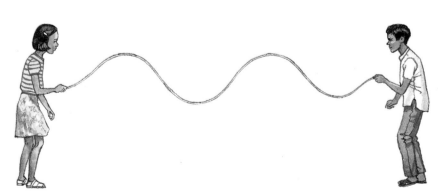

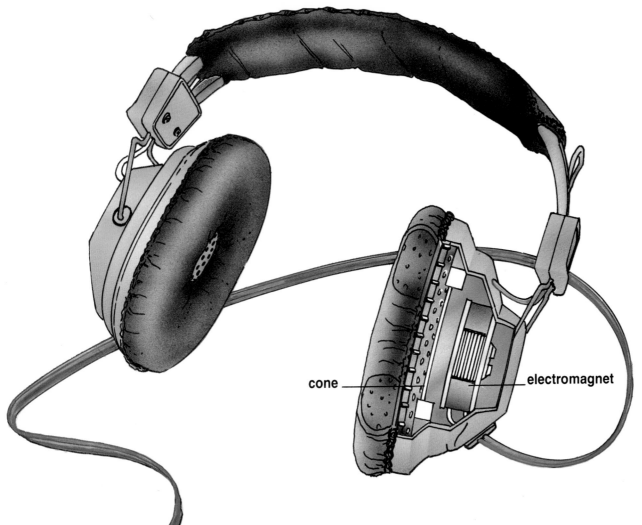

cone — electromagnet

signal to amplifier

Amplified sound signals are fed from the radio into the headphones. Inside the earpiece, the cone vibrates and produces sound.

Changing the signal to sound

The last stage in the journey of the radio signal from the transmitter to your ears is through the speaker or headphones. Here the radio signal is turned into an electric current. This is then turned into a sound that you can hear.

Amplified signals are fed into the speaker or headphones. Then they travel around a coil of wire called a **voice coil,** which is wound around a magnet. A **cone,** usually made of paper, is attached to the voice coil. The electric current from the radio signal passes through the coil and through the magnetic field produced by the magnet. The electric waves flowing through the coil cause the cone to vibrate, producing sound waves imitating those that first went into the microphone.

If you have a stereo radio and are listening to a stereo broadcast, the radio has to amplify and deliver two separate sets of signals to the speakers or headphones.

Find out more by looking at pages **94−95**
96−97
100−101

*This **circuit board** from a radio shows how the transistors are connected to other parts. The board has a printed metal circuit instead of wires.*

Inside the amplifier

In 1947, the **transistor** was invented. This invention has made it possible for us to carry small radios about. A radio has an antenna which picks up signals. These signals are radio waves which are broadcast by a transmitter. As they travel through the transistors, the signals are amplified. The amplified signals are fed to the speaker or headphones.

How transistors work

Transistors control the flow of electric current inside a radio or an amplifier. From the outside, a transistor looks like a small metal button with three legs. Inside the metal top is a tiny **silicon chip.** This is made of pieces of two types of crystal, arranged in a sandwich. The crystals carry electricity in different ways and are called **semiconductors.**

The parts of a transistor

A transistor has three connections—the base, the collector, and the emitter. These three connections are joined to a battery or a source of direct current. A weak signal is fed into one connection, usually the **base.** Most of the energy from the power supply flows in through the **emitter** and makes the signal stronger. This amplified signal then comes out through one of the other connections—usually the **collector.**

This drawing shows the main parts of a transistor.

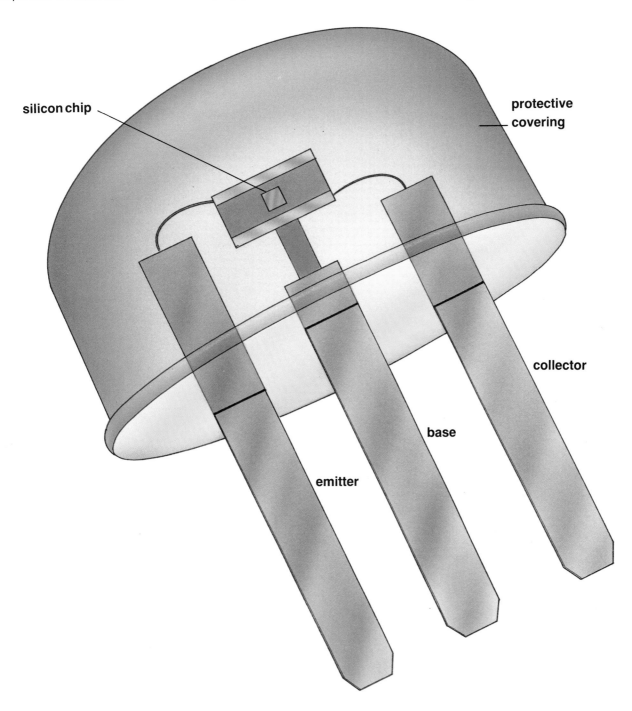

silicon chip

protective covering

collector

base

emitter

Smaller and smaller

There is little room to spare inside a space vehicle. Every pound of extra weight makes it more expensive and difficult to put a spacecraft into orbit. But a spacecraft carries hundreds of pieces of electronic equipment. As the first rockets were launched into space, it became important to find ways of making equipment smaller.

Scientists in the United States of America had the idea of putting electrical components on one piece of a semiconductor material, called **silicon.** The items needed to carry out a number of different jobs were thus made in one piece, all mounted on a tiny strip of semiconductor material. The entire piece was known as an **integrated circuit.** The first integrated circuit was patented in 1959. Today there are some circuits that are less than .08 inches (2 millimeters) square and may contain thousands of parts, or **components.**

These astronauts fly their spacecraft with the help of electronic equipment powered by tiny integrated circuits.

Silicon chips

Integrated circuits soon came to be called **silicon chips.** They are less likely to be damaged because there are no wire connections between different components. If they go wrong, they can be quickly replaced. There is no need to take the components apart, find the faulty one, and put the circuit back together.

Integrated circuits are used in all kinds of equipment, from computers and calculators to wristwatches. Equipment made with integrated circuits can be small, light, and easy to use. Some telephones have integrated circuits which give them a memory. If you make a call and the line is engaged, the telephone "remembers" the number, and you can try again later by pressing just one button.

This integrated circuit has been magnified about 200 times. The components and connections are engraved on the surface of a silicon chip. The chip is enclosed in plastic to protect it.

The silicon chip is so small that it will fit easily onto your fingertip.

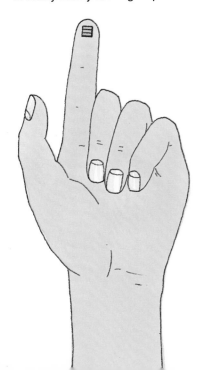

102

Find out more by looking at
pages **104–105**

The television camera

Radio turns sound waves into electric signals. These can
then be carried by radio waves from the transmitter to your
home. There the electric signals are changed back into
sound. Television works in the same way, but it turns
light waves as well as sound waves into electric signals.
These are then carried by radio waves.

The machine that picks up the light waves and starts them on
their journey is called a **camera.** But it is not like a photographic
camera, which takes one picture of a scene. A television camera,
though immobile, still takes thousands of tiny pictures of each
scene. It can also move across the scene in an orderly pattern
called **scanning.** A series of still images appears, one after the
other, on your television screen. This happens so fast that the
images merge together and what you see is a single, moving
picture.

*Sound is picked up by a microphone
and changed into electric signals.
The sound signal is added to the
picture signal before they both go to
the transmitter.*

*Light waves enter high-quality
color cameras and are separated
into primary colors — blue, red and
green.*

*These waves pass down three
camera tubes and hit three
signal plates.*

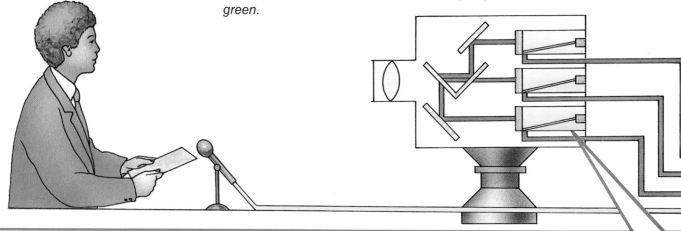

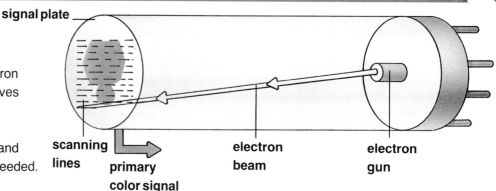

The camera tube

Inside the camera tube an electron
beam from the electron gun moves
across the signal plate. This
produces an electric signal for
each primary color — blue, red and
green. A total of three tubes is needed.

signal plate

scanning
lines

primary
color signal

electron
beam

electron
gun

Painting with light

If you were painting this scene, you could mix each color in the picture separately. The television camera scans the colors in the picture and separates them into blue, red, and green. At the same time, the camera scans the picture for brightness and depth of color. All this information enters the camera where it is turned into electric signals.

The control room of a television studio is where the program director chooses which pictures to send to the transmitter.

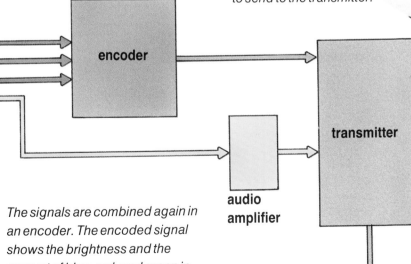

The signals are combined again in an encoder. The encoded signal shows the brightness and the amount of blue, red, and green in each of the thousands of tiny pictures.

Find out more by looking at pages **102–103**

Receiving television

Television signals can arrive at your home in three different ways. They may come along cables laid underground. They may come from a land-based transmitter which sends radio waves across the earth's surface. Or they may come from a satellite. Programs are beamed up from a transmitter to a satellite which beams them back to earth.

However, the signals arrive, your television set has the same job to do. It receives a jumble of information in the form of electrical signals. It has to sort these out and turn them into pictures and sound. First, the signal must be amplified by passing it through an electronic circuit. Then the sound and picture signals must be separated, the sound signal fed to a speaker and the picture signal fed to the television screen.

The television tube

The picture signal must reverse what the television camera did. It must build up a picture by scanning light across your television screen. This is done in the tube. A television tube is shaped like a funnel. At the open end is the screen. The back of the screen is coated with more than 300,000 dots of a chemical called **phosphor.** Phosphor glows in the primary colors when bursts of electricity called **electrons** are shot at the dots. At the other end of the tube are three electron "guns" that do the shooting.

Each electron gun receives the picture signal. This contains the information from the camera about the brightness and colors of the picture. It scans the screen with this information, just as the camera scanned the scene in front of it. This happens so fast that the viewer doesn't notice it.

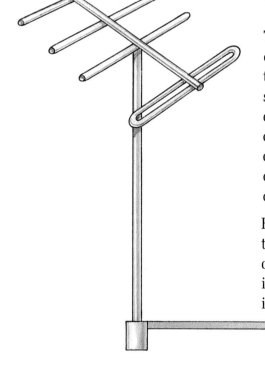

The TV antenna receives radio waves from the transmitter. The waves are turned into electrical signals. A tuner selects a signal which is then amplified and split into sound and picture signals.

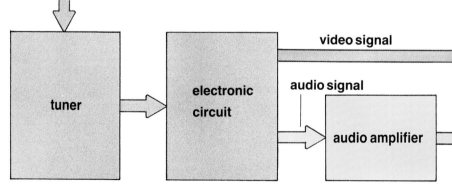

tuner

electronic circuit

video signal

audio signal

audio amplifier

Behind the TV screen is a metal shadow mask which has rows of holes. The screen is coated with tiny phosphor dots, arranged in groups of threes. These glow red, green, or blue when electrons are fired at them. Three electron guns fire electrons through the mask, so that each gun lights up the correct color.

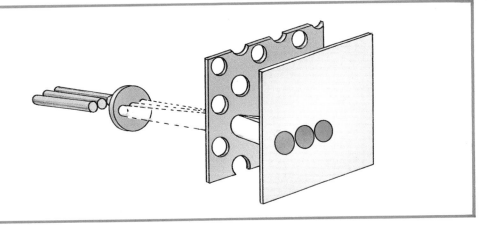

decoder

primary color signals

electron "guns"

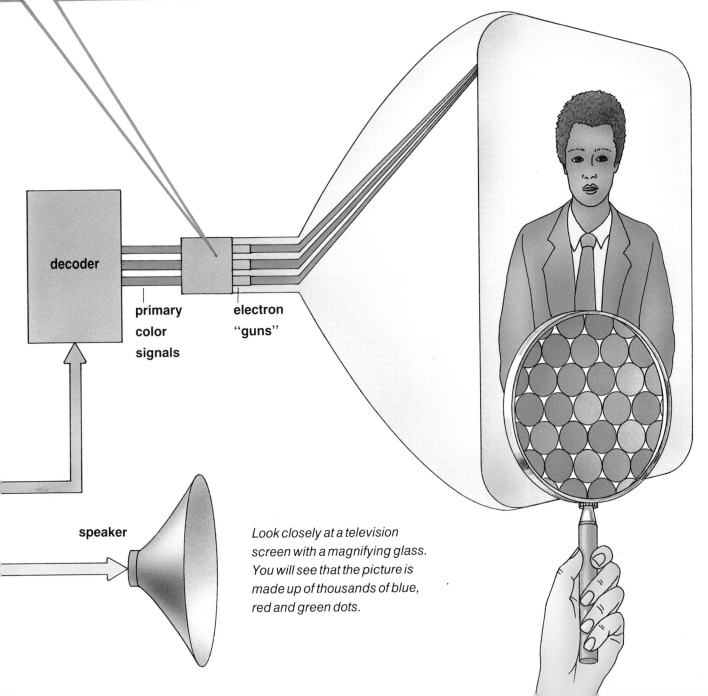

speaker

Look closely at a television screen with a magnifying glass. You will see that the picture is made up of thousands of blue, red and green dots.

Communications satellites

When a radio signal reaches a communications satellite, it is very weak. Before returning the signal to earth, the satellite amplifies the signal to make it stronger.

Messages sent by communications satellites are carried on microwaves. These electromagnetic waves can travel at a speed of 186,282 miles (299,792 kilometers) in just one second.

Solar power

Most satellites are powered by **solar batteries,** which make electricity from the light of the sun. Each satellite needs to be positioned so that rays from the sun are collected by its **solar panels.** Sometimes the satellite can make small movements to ensure that it stays facing the sun.

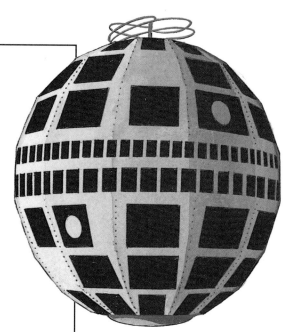

Telstar was the first satellite to send television pictures between the U.S. and Europe. It circled the earth every 158 minutes.

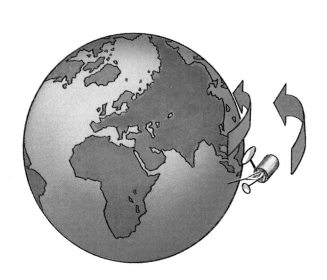

Geostationary satellites

Some satellites are **geostationary.** They seem to hover above the earth. In fact, these satellites are traveling in orbit with the earth. They remain 22,300 miles (35,900 kilometers) above a single point on the earth's surface because they travel at exactly the same speed as the earth rotates. Both satellites and planet take 24 hours to complete one rotation.

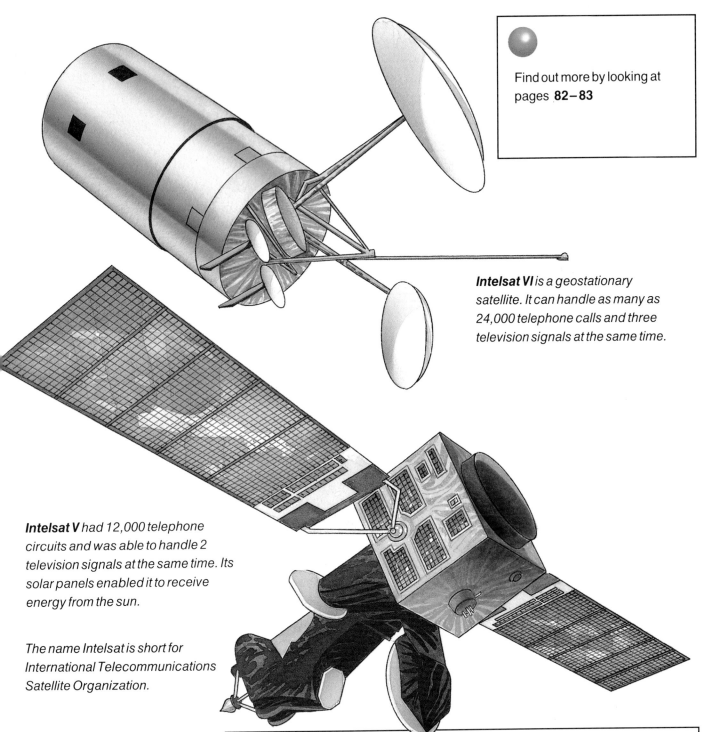

Find out more by looking at pages **82–83**

Intelsat VI is a geostationary satellite. It can handle as many as 24,000 telephone calls and three television signals at the same time.

Intelsat V had 12,000 telephone circuits and was able to handle 2 television signals at the same time. Its solar panels enabled it to receive energy from the sun.

The name Intelsat is short for International Telecommunications Satellite Organization.

Space rubbish

There are over 1,800 satellites circling above the earth. Only about 400 are still working. There are also many pieces of broken satellites and space rockets. These pieces are known as "space rubbish." This rubbish hurtles through space at a tremendous speed. A very small piece can badly damage a satellite.

Find out more by looking at pages **82–83**

Communications on the move

There are many people whose work involves traveling. Doctors often need to make or receive telephone calls while they are moving around. Every day, they are traveling between home, hospital, office, and other places. When they are out, someone may need to speak to them urgently.

Beeping messages

The doctor may carry a small **radio-pager.** If his or her hospital sends a radio signal, the radio-pager picks up the signal and makes a beeping sound. The beep means "Please telephone the hospital." As soon as possible, the doctor finds a telephone and makes the call.

Calling all cars

The police, fire, and ambulance services have their **two-way radios.** The link between the exchange and the radio is a radio transmitter. The exchange can relay calls from one transmitter to the next. These two-way radios work on special wavelengths, so that emergency messages do not get held up by less urgent ones.

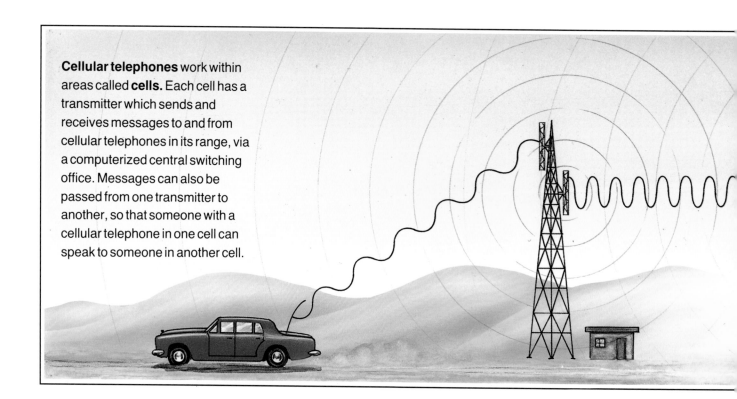

Cellular telephones work within areas called **cells.** Each cell has a transmitter which sends and receives messages to and from cellular telephones in its range, via a computerized central switching office. Messages can also be passed from one transmitter to another, so that someone with a cellular telephone in one cell can speak to someone in another cell.

Cordless phones

You can communicate while you are moving around in your own home. Many people have long extension cords on their phones or a number of phones in different rooms. But you can also buy a cordless telephone that you can carry in the house or out into the garden with you.

The cordless telephone has a base unit which is connected to the telephone line. It also contains a small radio transmitter and receiver.

When a call comes in along the telephone line to the base unit, it is transmitted by radio to the handset. When a call is made from the handset, it is transmitted to the base unit and then along the telephone line.

Leaving a message

We can speak to each other over long distances, thanks to the telephone. But how can we leave a message for someone who is not there when we call?

Modern telephone answering systems have a recording machine, which can be connected to your telephone. Sometimes the machine has a built-in telephone. When the telephone rings, the caller is connected to the answering machine. An automatic switch activates a pre-recorded message to which the caller listens. The message is recorded on tape and usually tells the caller to leave a message, name, and telephone number.

Once the pre-recorded message has played, the tape records the caller's message. This can be played back later through a speaker in the answering machine.

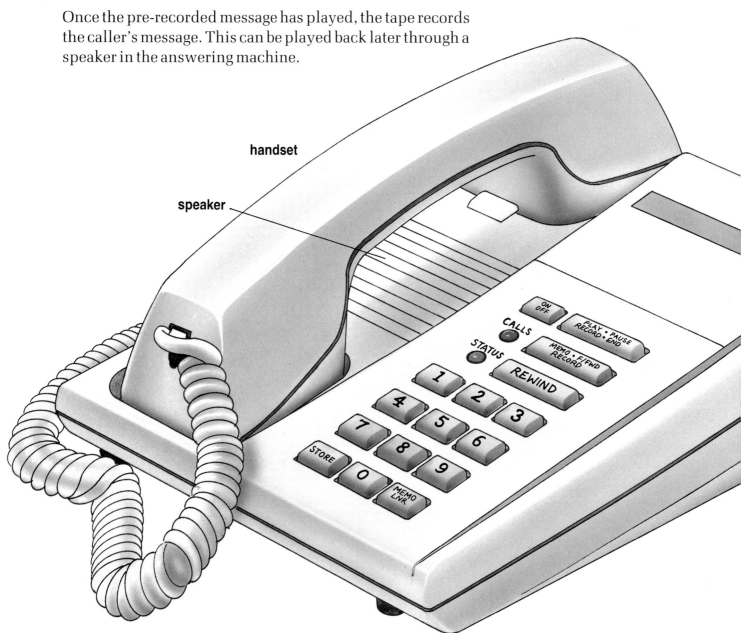

handset

speaker

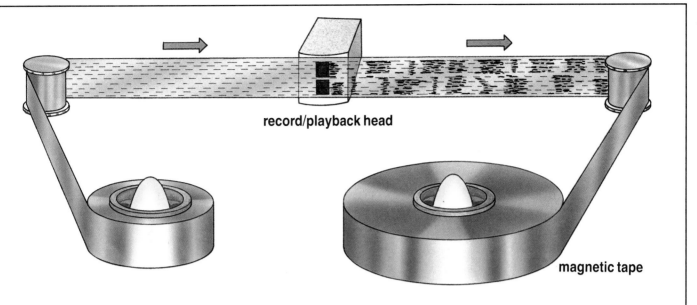

record/playback head

magnetic tape

tape machine

tape cassette

Inside an answering machine

Electric signals sent along the telephone line are passed on to an electromagnet called the recording head. A special tape is passed across the head. Signals from the head magnetize small particles on the moving tape. When this happens, the particles are arranged in patterns. These patterns are the stored form of the electric signals, and of the message.

To listen to the recorded message, the tape is passed across another electromagnet. This electromagnet, called the playback head, changes the magnetic patterns on the tape into electric signals. These are passed through an amplifier to make them stronger. They are then sent to a speaker which reproduces the sound vibrations and plays the message.

Messages by light

When electricity was first used for communication, it traveled along telegraph wires. Then came radio and television carried on radio waves. The newest method uses glass and light.

Have you ever held a magnifying glass over a piece of paper on a sunny day? If enough of the sun's rays pass through the magnifying glass, they can burn a hole in the paper. Light is a form of energy. Some watches and calculators are powered by the energy of light.

An optical fiber is about as thick as a human hair. Optical fibers are bunched together like electric wires to make cables that can carry thousands of messages.

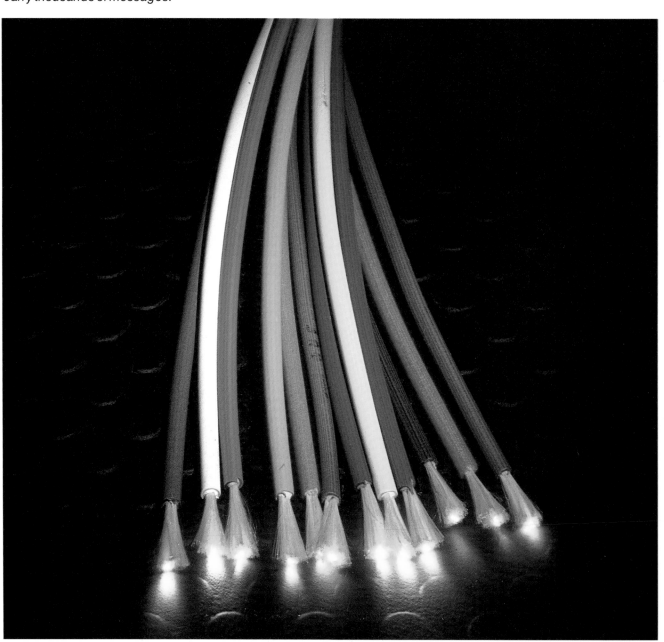

Laser light

In 1960, a new and powerful form of light was invented. A **laser** machine produces a concentrated beam of light that is many times stronger than the sun's rays passing through a magnifying glass. Because it is so strong and so concentrated, laser light can travel long distances.

Tubes of light

Like electricity, light is either on or off. So it can be used like electricity to send messages in bursts, or pulses, of energy. Laser light can travel down glass fibers, carrying messages from one place to another. The glass fibers are called **optical fibers.** They are so thin that they can be threaded through the eye of a needle! Optical fibers are now replacing wires for new telephone networks.

Optical fibers are better than wires in many ways. They do not suffer from electrical interference. Laser light signals are stronger than electric signals, so fewer relays are needed. An optical fiber can carry more messages than a wire.

An optical fiber cable is much lighter and smaller than the metal telephone cables.

Keeping messages secret

If you wanted to pass on a secret to a friend, how would you do it? You might whisper if you were in the same room, or pass a note. But if your friend was farther away, it might be more difficult. Telegraph and telephone wires can be "tapped." This means that other people can make connections to them and listen in. Anyone with a radio can easily listen in to messages broadcast over the radio waves.

The answer is to send the message in a way that can be understood only by the person to whom it is sent. You can use a **code**. There are many different types of code. Codes can be written using numbers or jumbled letters of the alphabet. You can code up a message by hiding it in the first or last letters of each word in a sentence.

Find the hidden code in this sentence:

His toe can mend, although he will limp.

You will need:

stiff cardboard

pen

scissors

paper fastener

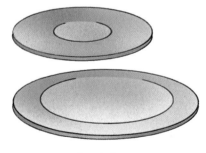

a saucer and a plate

Dial a code

Here is a simple coding machine that you can make. Each time you turn the inside card to a new position, you can make a new code.

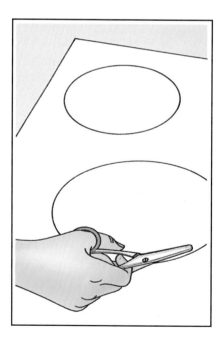

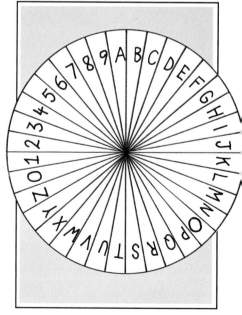

1. To make your coding machine, place the saucer and plate on the piece of cardboard. Draw a circle around each and cut them out.

2. Divide each circle into 36 segments. Placing one symbol in each segment, write the alphabet and the numerals 0 to 9.

Coded messages

Another way of sending a secret message is to split it up and mix it with other sounds. This is called **scrambling** the message. Only the sender and the receiver of the message know how to sort out the message, using a special machine.

Emergency code

Codes are used not only to keep secrets. Sometimes they are also used to pass information quickly. The letters SOS and the word MAYDAY are international distress codes. They mean that the sender needs help urgently. The emergency services respond quickly to these codes.

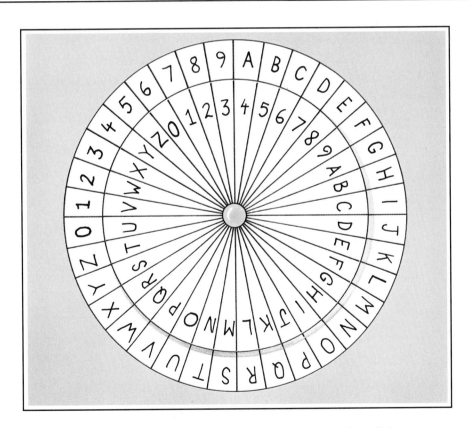

3. Place the smaller circle on top of the larger circle. Push the paper fastener through the center of both circles.

Now you are ready to dial your own code. Twist the top card so that A falls above 4. The code for HELLO reads B8FFI.

Jumbled letters

In another code, the letters of the alphabet are jumbled up. For example, "A" in the code stands for "Z" in the message.

Try making up some codes of your own using your name or favorite color.

A	B	C	D	E	F	G	H
0	1	2	3	4	5	6	7
I	J	K	L	M	N	O	P
8	9	**J**	**A**	**N**	**E**	B	C
Q	R	S	T	U	V	W	X
D	F	G	H	I	K	L	M
Y	Z	0	1	2	3	4	5
O	P	Q	R	S	T	U	V
	6	7	8	9			
	W	X	Y	Z			

Using the latest technology

Television was invented in the 1920's, and the telephone in 1876. But new ways of using these inventions are still being found, including cable television and "talking" by computer.

Television over cables

Television signals sent through the air are limited to a certain range of wavelengths. But if the signals are converted to a form that can be carried by **cable,** the range of wavelengths is much broader. A **cable** is a bundle of wires or optical fibers that carry pulses of energy, such as electricity or light. Like multiplexed telephone messages, many separate television signals can travel over one cable. This increases the number of possible channels from 13 to over 80.

A cable television company has a central station that picks up channels broadcast through the air and others bounced back to earth by communications satellites. It may also produce programming for several channels itself. It converts all these channels to signals that go out on a cable into the service area. The cable is split many times so that it can reach into individual homes where viewers pay for the service. In each home, the cable is connected to a converter device. (Some new television sets are **cable-ready;** that is, they do not need a separate converter.) The viewer uses the converter to choose a channel, and this device converts the signal to a form the television can use.

In cable television, programming channels are broadcast through the air or via satellite and then converted to signals to be carried by cable to the viewers.

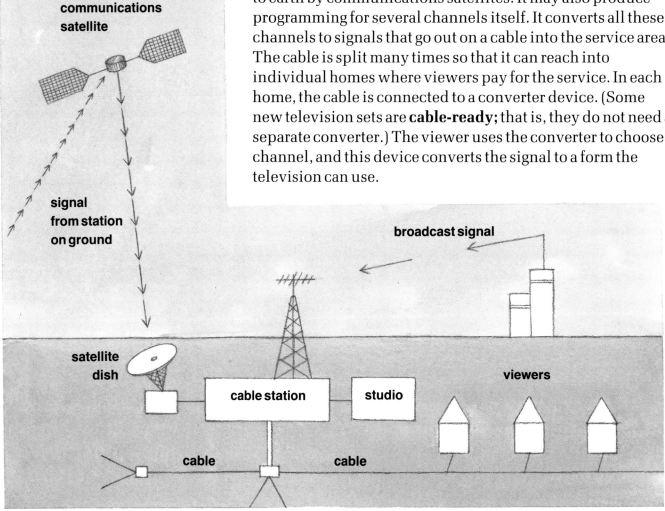

These two students are using a modem to access articles stored by an information service.

Messages through computers

Today many libraries, businesses, and homes have computers that can **access**—get in contact with—information services. These services offer up-to-the-minute weather and sports reports. They can find information that your library doesn't have. They have "bulletin boards" where you can leave messages for others who call in, and "mailboxes" where you can receive a personal message minutes after someone sends it. You can go shopping on some services. On others, you can play computer games with several people from different parts of the country—all together! Using a computer, a **modem,** and a regular telephone line, anyone can call such a service.

A modem—short for "modulator-demodulator"—is a device that **modulates,** or shifts, computer data into signals that a telephone line can carry. It also modulates computer signals traveling on the telephone line back into computer data. With a modem between a computer and a telephone, the computer can "talk" to another computer or to a service.

Glossary

Amplitude: Strength of a *radio wave.*

Antibody: Substance in a human being's or animal's body that fights disease.

Artery: Blood vessel that carries oxygen-rich blood away from the heart and to the rest of the body.

Axon: Longer branch of the *nerve cell* that carries messages out of the nerve cell. The axon connects with other nerve cells in the body and may pass their messages on to different parts of the body.

Bacteria: Small living thing that can live inside the body and cause disease.

Blood vessel: Tube through which blood travels in the body.

Cable: Bundle of wires or *optical fibers* that carry pulses of energy, such as electricity or light. It is used to send messages.

Cancer: Disease caused by cells that grow and divide without control.

Capillary: Tiny tubelike vessel in the body through which blood flows.

Cartilage: Smooth, rubbery substance that covers the ends of bones. It works like a cushion so that bones don't grind together.

Cell: Tiny unit of living matter that makes up all animals and plants.

Cytoplasm: Jellylike substance of which all cells are made.

Dendrite: Shorter branch of *nerve cells* that takes in messages from other nerve cells.

Dermis: Second layer of skin, where nerves and the sweat glands are found.

Digestion: Process by which food is broken down in the body.

Enzyme: Chemical in the body that helps break down food.

Epidermis: Top layer of skin.

Facsimile (fax): Device that sends and receives messages and pictures over telephone lines.

Frequency: Rate at which something vibrates.

Hemoglobin: Red substance in red blood cells that carries oxygen from the lungs to other parts of the body.

Hormone: Chemical substance that helps to control such body functions as growth, development, and reproduction.

Immune system: Network of cells that keep the body healthy most of the time by fighting invaders such as *bacteria* and *viruses.*

Joint: Place where bones meet. Joints make it possible for the body to move.

Kidney: Organ that filters waste and salts from blood. Kidneys make urine, the body's waste liquid. There are two kidneys, one on each side of the spine.

Laser: Machine that produces a concentrated beam of light that is many times stronger than sun rays passing through a magnifying glass. Lasers are used in medicine and industry.

Ligament: Strong, flexible strap that holds bones or other body parts together.

Liver: Body organ that removes some nutrients from the blood and stores them until they are needed. The liver also changes some nutrients into other substances that the body uses.

Marrow: Soft tissue in the hollow center of long bones. There are two kinds of marrow—red and yellow. Red marrow makes fresh blood cells and yellow marrow is mostly fat.

Microwave: Form of energy. A microwave is a superhigh frequency *radio wave.*

Nerve cell: Cell that uses impulses of electricity to carry messages throughout the body.

Nutrient: Any substance, such as food, that is nourishing and promotes growth and good health. Cells need nutrients to survive.

Optical fiber: Glass fiber so thin it can be threaded through the eye of a needle.

Organ: Part of the body that is made up of tissue joined together. Eyes, the heart, and the brain are examples of organs.

Periosteum: Strong substance that covers bones.

Protein: Food substance that helps the body grow and mend.

Protist: Soft, jellylike creature that invades the body and causes disease.

Red blood cell: Cell that carries oxygen from the lungs to the body tissues.

Reflex: An automatic movement that does not involve the brain.

Solar power: Energy from the light of the sun.

Spinal cord: Thick bundle of nerves that runs down the back inside the backbone and carries messages from the brain to the rest of the body.

Synovial fluid: Liquid that covers *cartilage,* keeping bones moving smoothly, like oil in the parts of a machine.

Telecommunications: Method of exchanging messages with the use of electricity.

Telegraph: Instrument for sending messages over long distances. It includes a key, which is used to send a message, and a sounder, which receives the message.

Tissue: Cells of the same kind and function joined together.

Transistor: Instrument that controls the flow of an electric current inside a radio, computer, and other electronic equipment.

Transmitter: Device used to send messages.

Vein: Blood vessel that returns the blood to the heart.

Vibration: Tiny movement of air that can be felt.

Virus: Tiny living thing that can live inside the body and cause disease.

Wavelength: Distance between the peak of one wave and the peak of the wave that is next to it.

Wave, radio: Electric signal that vibrates millions of times a second as it travels.

Wave, sound: Vibration in the air that makes noise.

White blood cell: Cell that kills germs that enter the body.

Index

Acknowledgements

The publishers of **World Book's Young Scientist** acknowledge the following photographers, publishers, agencies and corporations for photographs used in this volume.

Cover	Dr R. Clark and M. Goff, Hencoup Enterprises (Science Photo Library)
8/9	Michael Macintyre (Hutchison Library)
10/11	Secchi Lecaque (Science Photo Library)
18/19	Eric Grave (Science Photo Library)
28/29	Melanie Friend (Hutchison Library)
38/39	Spectrum Colour Library
42/43	Norman Myers (Bruce Coleman Ltd)
44/45	Will and Deni McIntyre (Science Photo Library)
46/47	Petit Format, Nestlé (Science Photo Library)
48/49	Science Photo Library
50/51	Biophoto Associates (Science Photo Library)
52/53	David R. Frazier
54/55	Martin Dohrn (Science photo Library)
58/59	St Bartholomew's Hospital (Science Photo Library); Bruce Coleman Ltd
60/61	Sunak (ZEFA Picture Library); D. and J. McClurg (Bruce Coleman Ltd)
64/65	Mike Surowiak (Tony Stone Worldwide)
88/89	Mary Evans Picture Library
98/99	Heini Schneebeli (Science Photo Library)
100/101	Astrid and Hans Frieder (Science Photo Library)
102/103	Adam Hart-Davis (Science Photo Library)
108/109	Motorola, Inc.
112/113	British Telecommunications plc; David Parker (Science Photo Library)
116/117	WORLD BOOK photo

Illustrated by

Sue Barclay
Richard Berridge
Farley, White and Veal
John Lobban
Annabel Milne
Jeremy Pyke
Gary Slater
Gwen Tourret
Pat Tourret
Gerald Whitcomb
Matthew White

Cover photographs

Infra-red waves were used to take this special photograph, called a thermogram, left. It is a visual record of the amount of heat given off by different areas of the skin, from the hottest (white) to the coolest (blue).

A tracking station, left, communicates with satellites and spacecraft throughout the solar system.